Surviving Grief . . .
and
Learning to Live
Again

Surviving Grief . . . and Learning to Live Again

Catherine M. Sanders, PhD

John Wiley & Sons, Inc.
New York • Chichester • Brisbane • Toronto • Singapore

This publication is designed to provide accurate and
authoritative information in regard to the subject
matter covered. It is sold with the understanding that
the publisher is not engaged in rendering legal, accounting,
or other professional services. If legal advice or other
expert assistance is required, the services of a competent
professional person should be sought. *From a Declaration
of Principles jointly adopted by a Committee of the
American Bar Association and a Committee of Publishers.*

Library of Congress Cataloging-in-Publication Data
Sanders, Catherine M.
   Surviving grief and learning to live again /
Catherine M. Sanders.
      p.   cm.
   Includes bibliographical references.
   ISBN 0-471-53471-4 (pbk.)
   1. Grief.   2. Bereavement—Psychological aspects.   I. Title.
BF575.G7S263 1992
155.9'37—dc20   91-43605
                                                                      CIP

Printed in the United States of America

10 9 8 7 6 5 4 3 2 1

Printed and bound by Courier Companies, Inc.

*I dedicate this book
To the wonderful people in the Tampa Bereavement Study
who, with broken hearts and spirits, willingly shared their
stories with me in the hope that they could be of some help
to others. My deepest gratitude goes to each one.*

Preface

When I was writing *Grief: The Mourning After,* my earlier book for caregiving practitioners, I kept slipping into sentences that were speaking directly to grieving persons rather than to the professional caregivers. I think I had already decided that a second, more personal book, written for those who are experiencing grief firsthand, could reach and help many more people.

I've drawn from a wide variety of resources to write this second book: my own research, therapy with bereaved individuals, and my personal experience with deaths in my immediate family. A large part of the information here is based on a research project I conducted in the Tampa, Florida, area. I met with 125 bereaved individuals who had lost a spouse, a child, or a parent. I followed each person through his or her first two years of bereavement. I met with each of them several times, and we usually became good friends. Throughout the book, I refer to my research project as the Tampa Study. The information gained from this study has given me valuable insight into the course of bereavement, and it is the cornerstone for the phases of grief I describe in Chapters 2 through 6. I call this whole approach the Integrative Theory of Bereavement.

Most of us don't know what grief is like until we lose someone we love, and no two experiences of loss are exactly the same. The closeness to us of the person who dies; the

time in his or her life—and in ours—when death comes; and
the unique circumstances of each death all make a difference in the way we grieve and in the length of time we take
to heal.

Grief's common denominator for us all, however, is pain.
When we lose a dearly loved person, we feel unbearable emotional pain. There is no getting around the pain; we must
move through it if we are to heal. Trying to avoid the painful
emotions of grief only leads to greater problems—illness or
serious chronic distress. Worst of all, avoiding the painful
feelings of grief leaves us psychologically stuck where we are,
unable to change and grow.

Grief is felt on many levels at the same time. Physically,
the symptoms include headaches, gastrointestinal discomfort, palpitations, dizziness, and, possibly, panic attacks.
Psychologically, the distress can be experienced as yearning,
crying, anger, frustration, and feelings of guilt and shame.
Social deprivation is another level of grief. When we lose a
significant person, we experience social isolation and alien-
ation because we see ourselves as different from others and
different from ourselves before the death occurred. When
our husband or wife dies, our roles in the community and in
our close circle of friends can change drastically.

What heals us finally? When we *actively* move through the
phases of grief, we work toward restoring a healthy perspective. We can't deal with grief passively; we have to participate fully.

Each of us experiences each loss of a loved one in a unique
way, often depending on how close we were to the person
during life and how prepared we were, together, for the reality of the person's death. Still, the best preparation cannot
protect us from the intense pain that follows the loss.

My prologue is a description of my own losses, across
three generations of my family. Read it, and you will understand that I do know a survivor's devastating pain.

I think it is important for you to know the level of your
own pain. Draw your own Self-Profile of Bereavement by

answering the questionnaire on pages 19–21. Put a date at the top of your answer sheet. A few months after you finish this book and actively put into effect the help I am offering, fill out the Self-Profile of Bereavement again, and compare your results against your present score. This will give you an idea of the progress you have made toward resolving your grief.

My book explains the complete process of bereavement. As survivors, you move through five phases of grief: shock, awareness of loss, conservation/withdrawal, healing, and renewal. You're in one of those phases now. When you understand those phases, it will become easier for you to move more calmly into each new phase. You may often wonder whether you're going crazy; this book will help you to accept grief as a natural experience. You'll see your reactions as part of a normal process that you must move through, to accomplish healing and renewal. The stress you are feeling will then be greatly reduced.

In surviving the death of someone dear, we face one of life's most agonizing challenges. We have the opportunity, once we have worked through the phases of grief, to surface as a stronger, more competent, new individual. The "working through" takes time, energy, and a persevering heart. Many times, we feel like quitting. In these times of loneliness and defeat, our courage is at its lowest. And yet, something carries us through: something, call it what you will—God, providence, or a higher power—gives us the strength to begin again. I believe that unless we can rely on some higher power to help us through the long and arduous journey of grief, we can't deal with the need to forgive, to love, or to fully belong to other important relationships.

In this book, I join the disciplines of experimental research and clinical application with spiritual dimensions. I am firmly convinced that grief deals with issues of the soul as well as emotional and physical issues. To understand the grieving process, it is important to be able to embrace all three.

My hope in writing this book is that you will understand that grief has a progressive course and that your grief will move through the steps of that course. Through all your pain, I hope to reassure you that you *will* survive and, in time, you will feel alive once more.

CATHERINE M. SANDERS

Charlotte, North Carolina
April 1992

Acknowledgments

First and foremost, I want to thank all the bereaved people who have contributed their stories, their suggestions, and their enormous courage and wisdom to this book: participants in the Tampa Study, patients who allowed me to share their journey, and the many other bereaved persons I have met along the way. Their stories are all here, although I have changed their names and shifted some of the situations surrounding the deaths in order to preserve their privacy and confidentiality. I am deeply indebted to each of them.

I am grateful to my daughter, Catherine Merrill, for her careful reading and professional comments as well as her strong support all during the writing of this book. How lucky I am to have a writer in my family.

To my long-time friend, Mary Howerton, I owe two debts of gratitude. Not only did she spend many hours scanning each chapter as I finished it, but she allowed me to use her beautiful poem, "Flight," which is in print for the first time. I appreciate having it become a part of this book because she has become a part of my life.

"Ours and Mine," another original poem, was written by my dear friend, Harold Boysen, shortly after the death of his first wife, when he was in deep grief. It is with a great deal of love and pride that I include his poem.

In Chapter 11, on mourning rituals, I have drawn extensively on the work of my good friend, Virginia Hine.

Virginia was a teacher for me in many ways, and I miss her deeply. I am grateful for the time we had together.

I am most appreciative of the interest, patience, and support I received from Herb Reich, senior editor at John Wiley. He was brave enough to attempt a second book with me, thank goodness.

Maryan Malone, of Publications Development Company of Texas, the manuscript editor for the book, did an outstanding job in adjusting the text to read more smoothly. I am fortunate to have had such an experienced and capable person handling this end of the production.

Particular mention goes to my office manager, Kay Burns, who typed all the drafts, deciphering my marginal hieroglyphics with amazing accuracy. I am grateful for her help.

Finally, appreciation must go to my daughters, Sue Labella, Sally Bowers, and Catherine Merrill, and to my sister, Mary McKinney, who encouraged and supported me all along the way. They shared the losses and the griefs that provided the springboard for the writing of this book. I am fortunate indeed to have such staunch fellow journeyers.

C.M.S.

Contents

To One in Sorrow

Let me come in where you are weeping,
friend,
And let me take your hand.
I who have known a sorrow such as
yours,
Can understand.
Let me come in. I would be very still
beside you in your grief;
I would not bid you cease your weeping,
friend,
Tears bring relief.
Let me come in—I would only breathe a
prayer,
And hold your hand,
For I have known a sorrow such as yours,
And understand.

Grace Noll Crowell

Prologue: An Autobiography of Grief

I was four years old when my Aunt Ada died. She was living in our home when she became ill with cancer. Mother nursed her through her long illness and was with her when she died. I don't remember any of these events but, from age four, I had an image of Aunt Ada lying in state on our sunporch, in a white wicker casket. The casket wasn't made of wicker, yet I retained that memory for many years without ever questioning the use of wicker as a casket material. Because we rarely talked about death in our family, I was a teenager before I asked Mother, "Is it true that Aunt Ada was buried in a wicker casket?" She laughingly assured me that it was not true. The fact that Aunt Ada's casket was white had confused my memory.

I did not look at my aunt in her casket nor did I attend the funeral. All the children in the family were quickly whisked away for some time in the country with close family friends. Children then, as now, were sheltered from "morbid sights" that might traumatize them. My mother had a realistic acceptance of death, for she had dealt with many family deaths herself, but that was the way things were done then.

There were no deaths in my immediate family until my father died, when I was eighteen. Two months earlier, he had been given a diagnosis of lung cancer. Although he became very ill, the words "cancer" and "death" were never heard, and the entire family spoke only in terms of his recovery. My parents had been separated since I was five and my father lived in another state. Yet, his three children were with him during his hospitalization. When he died, we were completely unprepared, and suffered shock more than anything else. We had been disengaged from him for such a long time that our loss was of a father figure more than of the man himself.

We had no guidelines to follow. My brother wanted to sit up all night with my father's body at the funeral home, but a vigil wasn't allowed. (The funeral industry has a tremendous control over our death rituals.) I remember being terrified when I stepped into the viewing room alone. I wanted to say good-bye, but I was not able to approach this silent, still body of the person who had been my father. I felt ashamed that I couldn't go near the casket, but it didn't occur to me to talk about my feelings with anyone. Death and one's reactions to it were simply not discussed. I accepted the rule that one must be very brave, and felt I had somehow fallen short of my duties.

I can only guess how agonized my brother must have been; he was much closer to Dad than I was. But he kept his reactions to himself like a young soldier. It was surely no coincidence that his first alcohol-related problems began a short time later.

After the funeral, our family went our different ways. Death did not touch me again for many years. Then it hit with all the force of an earthquake, and my life and my family's were changed forever.

When my husband's work took him to Florida, we moved there with our two younger children. Our two older daughters remained up north, one beginning work in New York and the other entering nurses' training at Massachusetts General Hospital in Boston. Our move left us feeling terribly fragmented, and we tried to compensate by doing things together.

Even with a busy life in our new home, I had more free time than I was used to. We hadn't yet made enough new friends nor had we become involved in the community. Jim, our son, was making a poor academic adjustment, after his transfer from a small private school up north to a large public school in Florida. I decided to enroll in some courses at the local junior college and chose subjects that were giving Jim trouble. Classes began for me the last week of August, and I plunged in determined to show him how tough school could be for some of us.

On Labor Day, we decided to stay home and enjoy our own pool, our dock, and our boat for water skiing. We would play it safe, away from highway traffic. I settled myself by the pool with my French textbook. Catherine, our youngest, went off with some newfound friends. Hersh, my husband, stretched out for a nap, and Jim, with a group of friends, fueled the boat and took off for some water skiing. I remember watching my tall seventeen-year-old walk toward the dock, and thinking to myself, "How well he is developing, filling out. How fine he is becoming." He had everything going for him. That was the last time I saw him alive.

Not more than an hour later, a strange boat careened toward our dock. As it drew nearer, I made out my son's best friend, standing up and shouting, "Get an ambulance— Jim's been hurt." (I get sick to my stomach again as I write this. Strange, how that awful fear and nausea still reemerge when I focus on details of that day.)

The freak accident was partly caused, we guessed, by Jim's poor eyesight. Without his glasses, his vision was roughly 20/200. Skiing behind our boat, he had made a wide swing when another boat was approaching from the opposite direction. We supposed that Jim spotted the boat too late. He dropped the ski rope and, as he slipped into the water, he was struck in the head by the oncoming boat. The impact was so great that a passenger in the other boat was hurled into the water. We didn't know it at the time, but Jim had sustained a massive cerebral hemorrhage and a broken neck. We waited for the ambulance and watched helplessly as various life resuscitative methods were attempted. We were in a confused blur, not allowing ourselves to believe Jim would die. I know he was seriously injured but somehow I didn't admit the thought that he would die. (How could he? Children don't die.)

When he was placed in the ambulance, he was intermittently breathing and his color was good. My husband and I jumped into our car and tried to follow close behind the ambulance, but we couldn't keep up. We arrived at the hospital emergency room a few minutes after Jim did. We raced toward the desk and asked for our son. When the nurse asked us to wait in a tiny examining room, a cold terror swept over me. Even then, I don't think I allowed the possibility of death to enter my awareness.

We waited about five minutes, alone, neither of us daring to speak, before a doctor appeared. He was a young man, probably a resident; he seemed angry. His first question was, "What happened?" I quickly countered, "Never mind what happened. How is my son?" He answered without hesitation, "Your son is dead." Just like that. Not, "I'm sorry. We did all we could." No other words to help ease the pronouncement.

I couldn't move. I couldn't respond. I sat there numb, staring straight ahead, unable to comprehend the impact of what had been said. I don't know what I thought. I was plummeting downward on a roller coaster, with sights exploding on each other, and I was incapable of separating them or stopping the ride.

The doctor said a few words to Hersh and left. A nurse came in and said to me, "For God's sake, why don't you cry?" Would she have been more comfortable, had I broken down then? Ironically, she may have been the only person throughout the whole funeral who may have been made more comfortable by seeing tears. I later became aware of how afraid most people are of another's tears. I learned to keep mine to myself as I stumbled through my bereavement.

I asked the nurse if I could see Jim, but she didn't think it was a good idea. It would be better, she said, if I waited until he was at the funeral home. To this day, I have been sorry that I did not insist. I have since learned that the period immediately after a death is a most important time for good-byes. We were asked a name of a funeral home, I was given one sleeping pill, and we left. Empty hands, empty lives, changed, diminished, broken.

We were ill prepared, both emotionally and practically, to deal with grief. Because we had never thought much about death, we had no concept of the therapeutic aspects of a funeral home. Funerals, in our way of thinking, were barbaric rituals to be avoided whenever possible.

Years earlier, my husband and I had attended the wake of a five-year-old child of friends of ours. The little girl had been quite ill with a debilitating disease during most of her short life. When she died, it was heartbreaking to see such a valiant battle lost. Her parents were very brave. At the wake, the child was lying in a white casket, wearing a lovely dress that exactly matched the dress on the doll she held in her arms. The parents greeted each visitor unfalteringly and with immense courage. Not only did they have to live through the wake we attended, but they were planning a similar one the next day, in their hometown in Pennsylvania. We were incredulous that they would expose themselves to so much pain. We resolved that, if anything ever happened to either of us (God forbid we should even think about one of our children), we would have no wake and would make the funeral short and simple. We saw no gain in dragging out such an emotion-wrenching affair. How much we had to learn.

At the death of our son, with no experience or guidelines to follow, we fell back on that memory and the strong reactions we had experienced. As a result, we did everything wrong. Now, in retrospect, I can count the mistakes we made, one by one.

First, we decided to hold the funeral as quickly as possible. Perhaps we thought that once the funeral was over, some of the pain would be over as well and we would more quickly get our lives back together again. What we did, in fact, was exclude anyone who needed to travel any distance to get to the funeral—all our closest, dearest family and friends that we'd left in Massachusetts, the people who could have supported and helped us had they been there.

Our next error was not having a wake. We did not go to the funeral home at all, until the funeral; the memory of our friend's daughter was still too strong. The evening before the funeral, all Jim's friends gathered at the funeral home, without us, to pay their respects. Not one person was there to help them with their grief and this was probably their first death experience. In not joining them and sharing their loss, we perpetuated the denial of grief, truncating our bereavement and theirs even further.

Our third mistake was to have a private funeral. In our confusion and anger, we felt that it was important to "protect" all the teenagers who had been involved in the accident. After all, we thought, grief is really a private matter anyhow. What we failed to realize was that Jim's friends needed to mourn their loss too, and the ritual of a funeral serves this purpose. By having a private funeral, we excluded all those who needed permission to grieve, and we blocked out our opportunity to benefit from their support. We even told our daughter, Sally, then in nurses' training, not to come home; we said it would not be wise to interrupt her studies. It took Sally several difficult years to resolve her grief and to make real an event that happened so far away.

It's hard to imagine how we could have made such serious blunders. I can only say that, with our limited knowledge of death and mourning, we had no guidelines to follow. When death is upon you and suddenly your world comes crashing about your head, it is nearly impossible to make rational decisions. This is why it is important to develop firm convictions about funeral arrangements ahead of time. Sudden deaths do not provide planning periods.

The months and years that followed convinced me that our treatment of our grief and mourning had made our bereavement unnecessarily hard to live through.

After Jim's death, each member of the family withdrew into a separate compartment. His name was rarely mentioned, but his presence was like a huge boulder sitting in the middle of the house. Hersh and I blamed each other in ways we could not articulate. Catherine, so young, was left on her own to manage the terrible agony of losing her wonderful older brother.

I plunged into a frenzy of activity. I had always worked through tough times this way in the past; why not now? My compulsive self-reliance had never become more active. Continuing my classes, I often had to wear dark glasses to hide my tear-swollen eyes. My church work took on new momentum as I tried to show by "witnessing" that God gives us courage. I don't know how I did it, but I sang a solo in church two months after Jim's death. By April, seven months after Jim's death, I was exhausted and filled with despair. I had cried and grieved, but I had done it privately in my room or while driving my car. I would scream and sob until I pulled to a stop light where other drivers could see me; then I would compose my face until the light had turned green and I could move forward and sob again.

By April, the stress of grief had caught up with me. I became almost catatonic. Our physician, a former flight surgeon, diagnosed my condition as "battle fatigue." My need to withdraw and conserve energy was possibly the most frightening aspect of my bereavement. In our society, where depression is greatly feared but broadly experienced, we tend to avoid retreat. We fear that we might become emotionally ill if we sequester ourselves or surrender to our emotions. For the bereaved, however, withdrawal is necessary to heal the body after the emotional trauma of loss. Just as one must conserve inner resources and withdraw when recuperating from any physical assault, so the bereaved person needs the protection of a period of quiescence and retreat.

Indeed, I was to need all the energy and understanding I could muster; in the next decade, my family faced death repeatedly. We developed an expectancy of death that gripped us each time the phone rang in the late evening hours.

All the while that we were battling to survive Jim's death, my sister-in-law was fighting for her life against cancer. She had had two mastectomies, and each time she came out of surgery, she felt confident that the cancer had been stopped. She and my brother had never been able to have children.

They lived for each other. When the cancer metastasized to her spine, her illness became the focal point of their lives. Because they lived in another part of the state, they did not have the support of family and, of necessity, they withdrew from their circle of active friends. When she died, my brother was devastated; his world collapsed. Everything he needed was gone: his love, his best friend, his child, his comforter. He came to be with us four months later, at Christmas. Two days after New Year's, he died in his sleep, from pneumonia and alcohol abuse. With his wife gone, he had lost his will to live.

It was at this time that I became interested in studying bereavement. What caused the awful pain? Why does it take so long to get over a significant death? The psychological literature was not prolific, but what I learned propelled me into committed research. The work of other researchers showed a high death rate among bereaved widowers; in fact, there was a significant rate of illness and disease among bereaved people in general. But the most compelling fact that was uncovered in my immediate search was that very little information about bereavement reactions was available. In this area of so much pain and suffering, very little research was being done.

The following Christmas, our daughter, Sue, and Ben, her husband, visited for the holidays. Sue was six months pregnant with their first child. Ben was a thoracic surgeon doing a two-year military stint at Valley Forge Army Hospital. I was well into data gathering for my bereavement study by that time, which meant I was often interviewing bereaved individuals. I also needed a control group—people who had not experienced grief in the prior five years. Sue and Ben completed questionnaires and became my first control subjects. They were enthusiastic and supportive about my project. Ben, who faced death and grief in his work, was particularly encouraging.

In early February, Ben received orders to go to Korea. We rejoiced that he wasn't being sent to Vietnam. There was no fighting in Korea then, or so we thought. Besides, Sue could be with him and have her baby there. Only ten days after Ben arrived in Korea, there was an incident in the demilitarized zone, and a number of U.S. soldiers were wounded. Ben was assigned to the medical unit that responded. One severe thoracic injury was reported, and Ben, being the kind of physician he was, jumped aboard the evac helicopter so that he could give in-flight attention to the wounded man. All the wounded were loaded aboard. Shortly after takeoff, the helicopter was shot down. All crew and passengers were killed. Sue called from Pennsylvania that morning, her tiny voice, half-paralyzed with shock and fright, simply saying, "Ben's dead."

Again, grief was upon us, but this time it was different. We were agonizing for our daughter's loss while trying to provide support where we could. In the three weeks it took for Ben's body to be returned for burial, two memorial services were held, one in his hometown in Ohio and one in New York City, where he had completed his residency. We were with Sue constantly, all the while wondering how she and her unborn child would make it through. I remember positioning myself behind her as we stood by the open grave on a snowy March day, thinking that, if she should faint, I would be there to catch her. Her life force seemed to have been drained from her, and even carrying the coming child (or maybe because of it), she gave the impression that she would like to die too.

New grief always reminds us of old griefs. The pain that has diminished with time is revitalized and experienced anew, when we are again exposed to death. Watching Sue, I was reminded of my suffering after Jim died. We are especially vulnerable to grief at night, and waking from sleep in the dark is like a nightmare. I couldn't bear for Sue to wake to her aloneness, so I slept with her for the first month of her mourning, so that someone would always be near. Grief teaches us in little ways.

After prolonged rituals, we returned home to Florida to await Sue's child. What a strange juxtaposition. A life had stopped, a new life was waiting to begin. Sue cared little about anything, too caught up in agony to think about the future.

But think about it or not, the future pushed through one April morning when a tiny and beautiful baby girl was born. She was a gift of new hope and new life, a nurturing object for Sue's love. Sue's bereavement lasted for several years but was greatly ameliorated by the advent of little Kerstin.

Out of necessity, I dropped the bereavement study for the time being. It was impossible to think of interviewing grieving individuals with death so close to us all.

We don't learn to grieve through experience. Our grief doesn't make our next grief easier, and our last major grief probably will be as traumatic as our first. But we do learn some things through experience. We learn of our needs, and we learn how to be a little less confused and disorganized during the ritual days and even beyond.

Five years after Ben's death, my mother had a stroke. This had been her greatest fear; the thought of incapacitation was a kind of anticipated hell for her. At 81, she had maintained a vital and active life that would have left most 60-year-olds exhausted.

When the stroke occurred, she grabbed the phone, and, although she could not speak coherently, she kept making sounds into the mouthpiece until the rescue squad had located her house and broken in to help her. An emergency call reached me at the university, and I got to the hospital in St. Petersburg about an hour later. Mother was still on the stretcher in the emergency room. My heart broke as I saw the distinct stroke symptoms—sagging face, and inability to focus or to speak in anything but racing jibberish. Yet, she was alive and conscious, and I could even understand a word from time to time. What a tremendous relief. I thanked God.

Just before her stroke, Mother had spent Thanksgiving with us. Early on the holiday, we had gotten up to put the turkey in the oven and share a quiet cup of coffee together. The conversation turned into a life-review for both of us, as we relived many of our family memories. We eventually came full circle and talked of our deaths and of what we would like in the way of funerals and burials. This was not a morbid conversation but one of open and sincere sharing. We agreed that, if either of us had a serious illness diagnosed, we would be completely honest with each other in sharing that diagnosis.

I thought of that close time together, only four days before, and I knew that I needed to talk to Mother about what had happened to her so that there was no doubt in her mind about her present illness. When I arrived at the hospital the next morning, I became aware for the first time of the incapacitating seriousness of her condition. I could see the full extent of her left-side paralysis and hear her garbled speech and her inability to focus. Sadly, I realized the change that this vital, energetic woman would have to live with. Even with prolonged therapy, she would have grossly diminished functioning.

I remembered mother frequently saying, "When I can no longer drive my car, I want to leave this world." As thoughts like these raced through my mind, I couldn't hold back the flood of tears and I left the room to cry alone in the hall.

When I had composed myself, I knew I needed to uphold my end of the agreement we had made. Returning to her room, I said, "Mother, do you know what has happened to you?" She answered brokenly, "I fell." I realized that she didn't fully comprehend her situation; she didn't know that she had suffered a stroke. With some trepidation, I said, "No, Mother, you have had a stroke," and quickly added, "With physical therapy, you can come through this. Everyone feels that you can make it. I do too." Silently, I was saying, "Please try; please, for me."

Now, when I look back on that moment, I think it was then that Mother made her decision to die. The worst thing that she felt could happen to her had happened, and I truly believe that she chose not to go through the long, arduous process of surviving a paralyzing stroke. She did not respond to my statement nor did she attempt to talk with me again. From then on, we communicated through hand squeezes only, and she never opened her eyes again.

My sister, Mary, arrived from Lake Placid, New York, and we provided support for one another. Mother acknowledged Mary's arrival with a hand squeeze but I believe now that she had already started on her death trajectory.

By Thursday morning, the hand squeezes had stopped. Mother was comatose. I took a long, hard look at her situation and at my grief. How could I part with her? Yet, I could never wish for her to live in a state less than the one she had known before the stroke, and I knew she would not wish it. As the day wore on, I became more convinced of the diminished quality of Mother's life. In the late afternoon, I went downstairs to the little interdenominational chapel. On my knees, I released my mother into God's keeping. I would not hold her back if it was time for her to go. (But neither would I be less than exuberant if she could make a full recovery.) Within a half-hour, my mother died quietly, her breath slowly spinning from her lips, her decision carried through.

Mary and I stood in the serene, still, dimly lit hospital room saying our silent good-byes. Each of us felt Mother's warm and gentle presence, and each of us offered a prayer of thanksgiving for her easy passing and blessed release.

Mary finally turned and said, "I guess we should notify the nurses." No sooner had this been done than all hell broke loose. A code signal was sounded and the resuscitation team came running from all directions. There was no stopping them. I screamed, "My mother died the way she wanted to," but I was pushed from the room. The attending physician could not be located for at least an hour. By that time, Mother was on a respirator, forcibly breathing again. I thought, "Dear God, now she has to die twice."

Fortunately, our doctor was humane and understanding. After discussing the remote possibility of a qualitative recovery, he said he would concur with our thoughts and take her off the respirator. Mother died a second quiet death a few minutes later.

The death of a parent is a significant loss for children at any age. What amazes me is how little credence is given to those who grieve over the death of an aged parent. Few people recognize the enormous pain involved when an attachment figure of a lifetime is lost. I learned this throughout my bereavement for Mother. Inquiries about how I was feeling and any mention of Mother dropped off after the first week. People who did not know Mother asked the inevitable question, "How old was she?" When I answered 81, there was usually a shrug and a comment in the nature of, "Well, she lived a long life, didn't she?" as though she may have even stayed too long.

In the deaths I had experienced before Mother's, I found that I had to deal with one particular paradox. This involved walking out of a hospital after the death with nothing but a small bundle of clothing, and then later seeing the beloved one in a casket at the funeral home across town. A broad jump in perception was required. The time period not accounted for left a gap in the continuity of events.

In the late afternoon, waiting at the hospital for the funeral home attendants to arrive, Mary and I talked about this gap and how uncomfortable it had always made us feel. On the spur of the moment, we decided we would ride with mother in the hearse rather than walk out of the hospital and leave her to go alone. (Death might mean that others think of "the deceased," but it takes a while for the close family to realize that fact. She was still very much "Mother" to us.)

When the attendants were approached with our request, they reacted with confusion. "I don't think it is allowed. No one has ever asked that before." I kept insisting. "I'll check with my boss," one attendant said. Returning in a few minutes, he reported. "Mr. Smith said he would send a car for you." I responded, somewhat annoyed, "We have plenty of cars here that we can use. We want to ride with Mother. It's like going the last mile." They argued further but we stood our ground. "Look, it's only a few blocks anyhow," I said.

"We promise we won't break down or do anything out of the ordinary. How could it possibly hurt?" Finally, we were allowed to ride in the front seat but not in the back where we would have preferred. (It is strange that we pay enormous prices to care for our dying and dead, but we have little control over what is done.) Riding in the hearse with Mother's body lent some small peace to our grief. As we watched the attendants remove the gurney from the hearse and roll it through the doors of the funeral home, we somehow felt more complete. We had done something a little extra to express our devotion.

From previous deaths, we had learned the importance of open sharing during the funeral. Mother's funeral, held in our family church, was a celebration of her life. There were readings from her favorite spiritual passages; a dear friend played the organ for the service and another sang a well-loved solo. A piece was read that Mother had written herself, only three weeks before. I had found it tucked in her Bible the day after she died. It said:

This is the 12th of November and I awoke to a new world,
for every day is a world made new. Must meet new faces,
    new experiences
and be equal to giving my best to all.
Have just finished a book "The Greatest Faith Ever Known,"
    and it
was beautiful but it made my heart ache. The suffering was
    unheard of in
our world today. But the devotion to the cause is some-
    thing to
make us think. The love of God is the determining factor in
    our lives—
how we love Him and support His cause.
This makes one or breaks her.
What can I do today? I know not what the day may bring,
    but I shall
do what comes to hand and meet every experience with my
    best—
whatever that may mean.

There were tears, but a feeling of love lay like a blanket over the entire service, and we came away uplifted by the experience. There is power in rituals.

In 1988, Herschel, my husband, died. We had been divorced for three years, but it had been only a paper divorce. We had remained bonded friends, spending holidays together with our children and keeping in close communication by phone.

We didn't expect his death. Except for his emphysema, he was a strong, healthy man. His shortness of breath kept him from being robust, as he had always been in the past, but he had learned to live with that. He still exercised and walked his beloved beach. In retirement, Herschel had turned into a first-class beachcomber.

We celebrated Christmas 1987 at my sister's home in Lake Placid. After the holidays, a lingering cold kept Herschel feeling weak and lethargic. We didn't realize how deadly his condition could become.

Herschel's breathing became more labored as he tried to care for "the cold" at home. Eventually, however, he made an appointment with his doctor. As soon as the doctor listened to Herschel's chest, he rushed him to the hospital for immediate treatment for pneumonia—a dreaded disease when one has emphysema.

Treatment went well and Herschel was released in two weeks. He felt a bit stronger and was ready to recuperate at home. The antibiotics had done their duty, or so we thought.

Back in his home, he didn't seem able to recapture his usual strength and vitality. Instead, he grew weaker and went back into the hospital. X-rays showed nothing, but there was a blockage of some sort. A bronchoscopy was performed. Nothing. A needle biopsy was done (Herschel was too weak by then for surgery). Negative. His breathing was becoming quite labored. Oxygen was being given by the respiratory therapist at regular intervals throughout the day and night.

Our daughters had already arrived from various parts of the country; still, no one knew what was happening.

Herschel was exhausting himself with each word he spoke, and it took too much energy for him to write out what he needed. The girls and I felt a creeping terror as we sat by, helpless and unable to do anything. In an agonizing moment, Herschel told us that he feared suffocation. After that, he allowed us to take turns staying with him around the clock. I say "allowed" because, until then, he had been determined to be as independent as possible. We were glad to be there. We didn't want to miss any opportunity to be with him, and we certainly didn't want to leave his care to strangers.

Two days later, and only ten days after his second hospitalization, I came "on duty" at 6 A.M., relieving Catherine, our youngest daughter. Herschel had had a bad night. The hours had dragged by slowly, and Herschel was gasping for air. Around 9 A.M., he stirred, opened his eyes, and with labored gasping, said, "I've had it. Can't get better. Don't want to suffocate. Want to be—put to sleep. Get—the doctor—now. Ready to—go. Stop—all—treatment."

His eyes were frantic as he lay back on the pillow. He had given me orders and I was expected to comply. It didn't occur to me not to.

Fortunately, we were in a small private hospital where the physicians were sympathetic and humane. They listened to Herschel and agreed with his decision. All treatment was ceased and the nurses began each hour to alternately give him morphine and Valium.

Soon he began to relax and breathe a little easier. Sometime later, he opened his eyes and, with a small smile, said brokenly, "Wouldn't it be something if what they gave me to kill me made me better." Even at the last, his sense of humor didn't leave him.

Before Herschel closed his eyes for the last time, we were able to tell each other how much we loved one another. I asked him to wait for me; I said that I would be along when it was my time. He smiled and nodded a promise.

We kept our vigil in his room throughout the night. Only the nurses entered, with their hourly shot of morphine and

Valium. The girls and I meditated together from time to time, silently reflecting on his life and our lives together. What a holy and special time for us in that hushed hospital room. We wept intermittently, hugged and supported each other, and were able to individually say our good-byes to this wonderful, courageous man who had been husband and father to us.

A few minutes after 11 A.M. the next day, Herschel took his last breath. He died as he had lived, always able to make decisions for himself and to be in control of his life. I was proud of the way he had courageously faced death when he felt he had no other choice. A later autopsy revealed a massive cancerous tumor in his lungs which had metastasized to his trachea, weakening him and cutting off his air supply. His time would have been short anyhow, and he would have had a horrible death of suffocation, had he not requested that he "go to sleep."

Herschel and I had discussed our wishes for funeral and burial many times. We both wanted no open viewing, and cremation. We had decided that our ashes would be buried in the same grave in Tampa, next to our son, Jim, and Mother. We also wanted to be as involved as we could in the memorial service and the burial of ashes. We recognized that the more we could do during the ritual period, the easier our bereavement would be.

Every death is different. For Mother, death came swiftly and unexpectedly. Herschel's situation was different. We sat up with him for several days, maintaining a constant bedside vigil, before he decided to die. After his decision, our vigil became like a wake in many ways. We were given the chance to say good-bye, to silently reflect on his life and what he meant to us. We had a brief time to prepare ourselves for the years when we would be without him. We had assurance from Herschel that he no longer wanted to live. This was his choice and we supported him. The quality of life he needed was gone.

The memorial service was held in the small chapel of the church where we were married. The minister agreed to the participation of family and friends. He opened the service with a prayer, and the rest was done by us. Each family member or close friend who wanted to pay tribute got up and gave a short eulogy, adding special stories or underlining beloved characteristics that had special meaning to that person. It was one of the most moving, spiritually rich, and deeply emotional services I have ever attended. We all wept openly and unashamedly as we publicly said good-bye with deepest love and caring. Shared grief, I had learned, offers the most healing.

The ashes were not ready for burial for another week. By then, each of us had to be back in our home cities. We decided that burial would be done later. When I could arrange to go back to Tampa, Catherine and I conducted a private burial, using a ritual we devised on our own.

We were glad that we had been in charge of all preparations ourselves. As a family, we needed to agree on each decision before we went ahead with anything. Because we all had tasks that were important components of the whole, each person felt that he or she was doing something just for Hersh. We had not turned over the duties of the rituals to strangers. We had taken charge of the care and keeping of this dearly loved man.

What have I learned through a lifetime of losses? With Jim's death, I learned that we can't deny the pain of grief. We must accept the experience of pain in many different ways, but if we are strongly connected to another person, we will suffer.

With Ben's death, I finally understood the power of rituals and how they can help propel us through the early days of grief. They seem to be the glue that holds us together at the beginning of our grieving. Getting through the three services, a week apart, after his death, represented a focus for us. If we could make it through one service, we could get through another.

With Mother's death, I could see the importance of assuming more control in the death and burial of a dearly loved family member. Because we had little control over her care, we needed to participate in some other manner. By riding in the hearse to the funeral home with Mother, we felt that we were doing something special and sharing ourselves with her.

With Herschel's death, I learned that, when we assume a more participatory role in a family illness and death, our grief becomes easier to bear. By being open to death, facing it in a more accepting manner rather than fighting it, we feel less anger, less guilt, and, consequently, less pain.

I began my research into bereavement with one major question: How can we quell the pain of grief? I believe a partial answer might lie in a more confident acceptance of death as an important adjunct to life. If we could truly believe that death is a part of life and might be a happier part of life than life as we know it, we would become more accepting. If we keep our view of death as the worst punishment that could befall us, we will continue to deny, abhor, and fear death; to suffer the lengthy and painful bereavements we now endure; and to perpetuate the high illness and death rates that afflict bereaved individuals.

This has been my autobiography of my own grief. Looking back, I can trace my passage, however slow and painful, to healing and renewal. It's important that you understand your present level of grief and the degree of help or self-help you need. You may find that help solely in the chapters that follow, or you may find it necessary to seek additional professional counseling. Your score on the Self-Profile of Bereavement will help you to decide. As long as you actively work through the phases of your grief, you will, some day, look back on this time and see how far you have come toward your own healing and renewal.

SELF-PROFILE OF BEREAVEMENT

This questionnaire allows you to explore your own experience of grief. The statements below represent various thoughts and feelings commonly expressed by people who have suffered the loss of a family member or close friend through death. Read each statement. How well does it describe your reactions during your period of bereavement?

Directions: Alongside each statement that is true or mostly true for you, place a check mark (✓) in the space in the TRUE column. Alongside each statement that is not true or mostly not true for you, place a check mark in the NOT TRUE column.

		TRUE	NOT TRUE
1.	Immediately after the death, I felt exhausted.	_____	_____
2.	My arms and legs feel very heavy.	_____	_____
3.	I feel lost and helpless.	_____	_____
4.	I feel restless.	_____	_____
5.	I have feelings of apathy.	_____	_____
6.	I rarely feel enthusiastic about anything.	_____	_____
7.	Life has lost its meaning for me.	_____	_____
8.	I have frequent mood changes.	_____	_____
9.	Small problems seem overwhelming.	_____	_____
10.	At times, I wish I were dead.	_____	_____
11.	It is hard to maintain my religious faith in light of all the pain and suffering caused by the death.	_____	_____
12.	Life seems empty and barren.	_____	_____
13.	I seem to have lost my energy.	_____	_____
14.	I feel cut-off and isolated.	_____	_____
15.	I tend to be more irritable with others.	_____	_____

16. I often experience confusion.   _____ _____

17. Concentrating on things is difficult.   _____ _____

18. I seem to have lost my   _____ _____
    self-confidence.

19. I cry easily.   _____ _____

20. I often wish that I could have been   _____ _____
    the one to die instead.

21. There are times when I have the   _____ _____
    feeling that the deceased is present.

22. I sometimes have trouble believing   _____ _____
    the death has actually occurred.

23. I have the feeling that I am watching   _____ _____
    myself go through the motions of
    living.

24. I feel extremely anxious and   _____ _____
    unsettled.

25. The yearning for the deceased is so   _____ _____
    intense that I sometimes have
    physical pain in my chest.

TOTAL   _____ _____

To draw your self-profile: Total the number of check marks in each column. The number of your TRUE statements will fall into one of the following categories:

1 to 8   You are handling your grief very well.

9 to 14   There is need to take better care of yourself.

15 to 19 Find someone to talk with about your loss.

20 to 25 Seek professional help. You are holding in too
          much grief.

1

The Pain of Grief

Grief is so impossibly painful, so akin to panic, that we must invent ways to defend against the emotional onslaught of suffering. There is a fear that if we ever give in fully to grief, we would be swept under—as in a huge tidal wave—never to surface to ordinary emotional states again.

C.M.S.

When I began my research into bereavement more than twenty years ago, the major focus of my inquiry was directed toward learning how to quell the pain of grief. The loss of a loved one hurts so much. Not only is the intensity severe, but the pain appears to be as much physical as it is emotional. The emotional pain, I could understand; we have always heard about that. But I had trouble, at that time, believing that any physical pain could have a connection to grieving.

Since then, I have come to understand that we are probably unrealistic if we think we can avoid the pain of grief. Letting go of someone we love is not easy. The insecurity we experience following a major loss is frightening and debilitating. Yet, if we can learn more about grief and how it affects us, we can reduce the fear associated with grief's hurtful emotions. Reducing the resistance to pain often lessens the pain itself.

Most of us are taken by complete surprise when we encounter death. It is as if we expect life to produce all gains and no losses. Our expectations exist even though we know that we are going to lose some of our dearest loved ones along life's way. Do we still cling to childhood tales of a perfect world where everyone lives happily ever after? Perhaps that is why we are so rarely prepared for death.

Of all the people I interviewed in the Tampa Study, only a handful said that they were prepared for a death in even the smallest way. The others all said they were incapable of dealing with sorrow. They felt that what they were experiencing wasn't normal, that it was, instead, a form of mental illness similar to a nervous breakdown. Many said that it was more like fear than anything else.

I can identify with that description. When my son, Jim, died, the shameful sense that I was different from everyone else—that I must be a different person, inside and out, from the one I used to be—led me to a fear that I was going crazy. The thoughts and feelings I was having were foreign to me. I would rage at God, the doctors, and the rescue squad for not protecting Jim enough, and then yield to crippling guilt as I blamed myself for the same reason. These thoughts and feelings couldn't be seen by others. Yet, in my own mind, I was different. I had just lost my child.

WHY DO WE GRIEVE?

This might seem like a simple question, but few of us really understand much of grief's function. We grieve because our loss hurts so deeply. It awakens all our childhood fears of abandonment and leaves us feeling scared, exposed, and unsafe. We so dread facing our negative emotions that, at times, we avoid and deny the fact that we are feeling grief at all. I have heard people say, "I don't want to know anything about grief until I have to. It will find me soon enough." They're right; it will. However, if we are armed with an understanding of grief and know what to expect when it comes, we can face it more openly and less fearfully.

When we are separated from people we love, with no way to get them back and no way to fix things as they once were, we feel out of control and helpless. We miss having our loved ones near and ache to have them back. Intellectually, we know they are not coming back and yet it seems impossible to let them go. We remain in emotional conflict until we are finally able to release them. The major suffering of bereavement comes in this middle range of transition, after the ending and before our new beginning.

Denial: Not a Solution

Because loss is so painful, it is not unthinkable that grief is denied. The thought of separation from our loved ones fills us with as much dread as it did when we were children. Most of us can remember a time when our parents left us, even if only to go out for an evening, and we were inconsolable. Usually, our pain lasted only long enough for our parents to disappear from the driveway. Then our attention was turned to something else, a distraction of one thing or another. We often distract ourselves in grief, thinking that we are getting through it more easily. What we don't realize is that we must face our grief in order to come out on the other side of it. There is no other way. Distractions keep us occupied but don't move us toward resolution. We stay in a cul-de-sac, circling round and round, until finally we can bolt out onto the main highway once again and continue our journey.

Denial of grief is connected with the lack of traditional mourning clothing. Wearing "funeral black" may seem drab and old-fashioned, but in the past it carried a message of personal sorrow and an unspoken request for consideration from others. The message seemed to work both ways.

The comforters were alerted to show proper concern for the bereaved, and the bereaved, being comforted themselves, could respond to those who helped.

Another subtle aspect of denial has an effect on grief. There seems to be a cycle that confuses communication. It works this way: People are self-conscious and ill-at-ease in the presence of newly bereaved persons primarily because they have had so little to do with bereaved persons. The reason they have had little to do with bereaved persons is that they are self-conscious and ill-at-ease in their presence. To break this cycle, we need to begin at the beginning and remove the self-consciousness surrounding bereaved persons. It would be good to start with children, because they have a wonderful sense of compassion.

In the past, when death and grieving used to occur at home, children were taught death education naturally. They learned that mourners were in a special state of mind and required more consideration and more respect than they were given before the death. Most importantly, children were able to see how grown-ups acted during the rituals. They had good role models because people more openly showed their grief.

Today, children have few role models to imitate. Even worse, they are generally left out of the rituals of mourning—usually, to be protected from such morbid events. As a result, we have produced a generation that is unable to support bereaved persons. The denial of grief places a burden of silence on mourners during a time when they need to be nurtured and comforted. The art of condolence takes a special consideration that most people do not know how to give.

Excursions into denial are easy. We are always looking for distractors, for anything to keep us away from the pain. Yet, pain is exactly what we need to experience if we are to heal our wounded hearts. Grief is a strange paradox. We are forced to let go of our beloved persons at exactly the time when our souls are screaming to have them back.

Strong Attachments

Much of our grieving depends on the closeness of the relationship between ourselves and the one we have lost. Was it a child, a spouse, a parent, a friend? Each relationship carries a different meaning, different roles, and varying amounts of attachment. The closer the relationship, the harder it is to give it up.

Our attachments begin early in life. Shortly after we are born, we bond with our parents and an important connection develops. Sometime during our first year, we are able to establish a trusting relationship with them: we trust that they won't leave us. From that trust, we develop a gradual sense of security within our world. We feel that we can trust in other relationships. Our close relationships give us feelings of safety and security. Even our children, for whom we normally think we are providing the security, give us a feeling of completeness.

That's what attachment behavior is; it becomes a fundamental form of completeness and protection. When we lose a major attachment figure, we feel afraid and dreadfully insecure. The world becomes a frightening place. Everything that we have depended on is now turned upside down and we lose our way for a while.

Our Inescapable Feelings

The alternative to grieving is numbing ourselves so that we don't have to feel. This may seem like a less painful route at first, especially during the time when we are frightened and disoriented. Yet, to not feel means that we also give up joy, pleasure, peace, laughter, and all the emotions that we find most satisfying. If we have the courage to go into our grief, allowing ourselves to feel and experience both its positive and its negative effects, we can shorten the time it takes to survive a major loss. Only when we try to avoid the pain and escape the work of grief will we stumble and fall.

To get through our grief, we will need to know that it's acceptable to express our feelings. If we think we "have to be strong" and can express only positive feelings, then we won't be able to grieve. If we want to come out on the other side, with our grief work completed, then we need to give ourselves the permission, the time, and the acceptance to feel what we are feeling.

GRIEF AND IDENTIFICATION

In most close relationships, we take on the feelings of others, often experiencing them as our own. It is natural to identify with those near to us. This identification is especially true with our children. Actually, in many situations, we are more tuned in to what we think others are feeling than we are to recognizing our own feelings. If any member of our family expresses sadness or anger, we imagine what that person must be feeling and take some of it to be our own. If our husbands, for example, seem angry, we wonder what we have done to cause the anger and, as a result, often feel angry in response. If our children feel lonely or are left out of the group they normally associate with, we feel that loneliness also. This is identification. When we lose someone we have identified with, we lose a part of ourselves. The part of us that we shared with that person must now be cut off.

GRIEF WORK

Grief is exhausting. Few people realize that the work of grief takes a tremendous toll in psychic energy. This in turn affects our level of physical energy. If we were to do strenuous physical labor all day, we would reach the extent of effort grief requires.

Sigmund Freud was the first to use the term "grief work" to describe the mind racing and the inner turmoil that go

on when we are forced to give up a loved one. Our perceptions don't change easily. Once we have formed a reality
that seems true to us, we stick with it. It is difficult to
imagine that one day a person is here and the next day is
gone. When that person has been in our world as a significant figure, our perception is even harder to change. Because of our reluctance to give up a loved person, we have to
do it slowly, a little at a time. During this time, the period
when we slowly give up our beloved family member or
friend, much of the trauma of grief takes place. This is the
time when we feel our emotions most strongly—guilt,
anger, shame, frustration, and many other negative emotions. When we look at it this way, we can see that the term
"grief work" is most appropriate.

WHY DOES GRIEF HURT SO?

Grief has been compared to both a physical injury and a physical illness. It has also been called a psychological blow.
These definitions may all be accurate. We are aware that grief
can cause sickness and deep emotional distress. A number of
research studies have shown that there is a significant death
rate among widowers, especially during the first two years of
their bereavement. My own study indicated that people get
sick more often, following a major loss. Other studies have
shown that illness occurs after other types of losses as well—
divorce, retirement, or loss of a body part. Grief hurts so
deeply because we are torn from something or someone we
love and, with the loss of that love, part of us dies too. Our
frustration pushes us to unrequited yearning. When we lack
support from our family and friends or are stigmatized by
our community, our grief becomes almost unbearable.

Separation Anxiety

Our attachment to the one who has died will determine the
amount of separation anxiety we feel. The stronger the

attachment, the harder it will be to let go. The real agony of
grief is that we must give up someone we have grown to love
and hold dear. The loss of a loved one takes away both our
feeling of connection and an important source of love. We
are left desperate, frightened, and lonely. Our yearning to
have our loved one back becomes a source of ceaseless agony.

Death's final separation causes the gut-wrenching pain of
grief. In a sense, the experience is like the amputation of a
leg. First, there is the shock of realizing that it is gone. Then,
we must deal with the raw torture of the exposed stump.
The pain grinds deeply into our bodies as we seek some
analgesic that will ease the throbbing. After the initial pain
has subsided, we deal with the slow healing process, making
sure that we pay close attention to the care and treatment of
the wound. At the same time, we are trying to find some
meaning in the tragedy of our loss. As we gain some
strength, we learn to walk on only one leg, stumbling, reel-
ing, and often losing our balance. Somehow, we manage to
get up again. Finally, we learn to use a prosthesis and, from
all appearances, we can get around as well as anyone else.
Yet, underneath, we are never the same person. The experience has changed us. If we are lucky, if we have worked
through the ordeal, learned from it, and grown from it, we
can come out of it stronger than we ever were before.

Frustration

A major source of the frustration we feel during bereavement is that we search constantly for our lost ones but are
never able to find them. We scan every crowd, looking for
their faces. So often, the back of someone's head will look
just like the one we have hoped to find and our hearts will
jump with hope for a moment, until we realize we are seeing someone else. Our disappointment is shattering. Each
of these experiences fills us with renewed anger, frustration, and bitterness. We feel out of control and impotent
because we can't change anything. Grief is filled with these

disappointing situations, and we are kept on an emotional roller coaster. Is it any wonder that bereavement takes so much out of us?

Need for Social Support

Another factor that causes grief to be painful is that, for the most part, we lack social supports that offer us comfort and nurturance. We must usually grieve alone. The death rituals are intended to offer some support, but, even as we go through them, we are expected to disguise our pain, hide our emotions, and keep a controlled demeanor lest we make others feel uncomfortable. More importantly, we may not want to embarrass ourselves by becoming too vulnerable and breaking down in front of others. Through most of my bereavements, I have been the one who comforted others who thought they had come to comfort me. This was my error. I had not learned to receive from others or to ask for what I needed. Our attempts at denial are actually aided by our friends and family, who are all too willing to go along with our "normal" behavior.

The Stigma of Grief

Bereavement carries a peculiar stigma. Because our society views death as the worst thing that can happen to us, a death is often seen as punishment not only for the one who died but also for the survivors. We feel victimized and penalized, as though a sentence had been handed down by some higher court and there is no way to appeal.

A number of people in the Tampa Bereavement Study talked about the isolation they experienced after a death in their family had occurred. "People would go out of their way to avoid me," one bereaved mother said. "It was as if I had a contagious disease." The stigma of death generalizes to the survivors, making them feel alienated and stripped.

As long as death is viewed by our culture as a failure, we, the survivors, will experience some degree of shame.

WHAT COMPLICATES GRIEF?

No two people will grieve alike. Besides, each of us has met grief in a different way. Some of us experienced our loss suddenly; perhaps our loved one was killed in an accident or died quickly of a heart attack. To others, death may have given ample warning that it was coming, and we thought we had time to prepare.

The way that death happens, where it happens, or to whom it happens will make a difference in how we process grief. The death of a child will generally result in a long and complicated bereavement for the parents. The shock of losing an integral part of themselves creates a reaction that continues painfully for a long while. The shock of seeing a loved one die often develops into chronic grief. Mrs. Hill was looking out her kitchen window when she saw her husband having his heart attack. He was dead before she could reach him. Shortly after the funeral, she developed crippling arthritis that didn't leave her for months. Hers was a long and arduous bereavement.

Sometimes, the events surrounding a death create situations with which it is impossible to cope. The pain is as intense as in all losses, but the circumstances are so disruptive that resolution becomes complicated. Coping mechanisms then break down and physical functioning is at a low ebb. These effects are felt by MIA families, survivors of victims of terrorism, and families of innocent bystanders murdered by crossfire or a senseless spray of bullets.

Sudden Death

Sudden death presents more symptoms of shock and consequent somatic problems than death that is anticipated. The mind has no time to prepare a rational explanation nor is there any opportunity to process feelings. The shock that is experienced reverberates through a survivor, causing an extreme assault on his or her physical state. As a result, the process of grief is slowed. Our bodies attempt to heal themselves in the aftermath of a sudden death. We don't have the emotional or physical energy to do the work of grief until we have regained the resources necessary for energy replenishment.

Ambivalence

The more ambivalence there is in a relationship, the harder the grief work when the relationship ends in death. All relationships include a certain amount of ambivalence. Whether in a marriage, a child–parent bond, or any other closeness to a family member or friend, we all know that no relationship is perfect. Problems in bereavement are caused when these negative emotions, such as hostility and guilt, surface after the death. They are usually repressed because it is not socially acceptable to show negative emotions at the time of a death. Unfortunately, they continue to stew, often surfacing much later, when we think grief is behind us.

Realistically, in most marriages and in most sibling relationships, there is usually a time when we have wished that the other person was simply not around. If that person dies, there is a tendency to torture ourselves with guilt and shame; we feel that we had something to do with the death. It takes a long time before these issues can be resolved, and they often tend to complicate bereavement. We need to forgive ourselves for the negative emotions that occur in every relationship and acknowledge that remembering them is a normal part of grief.

Personality of the Bereaved

We are all so different: no two people respond to grief in exactly the same way. But then, no death is exactly the same as any other. We all have different relationships, different life conditions. By the time we reach adulthood, our personalities are pretty stable and will usually dictate what our reactions will be when death takes someone close to us. If we are inclined to deny negative events or thoughts, then we will deal with grief in the same manner, never letting anyone see us cry or look sad. This "public face" may keep us from feeling vulnerable and out of control, but we invite a big problem because we risk never having any support. If others don't think we need consolation, they will be relieved that they don't have to offer it. They will think that our bereavement is over and that we are back to normal.

For those who already deal with stress poorly, such as those who have experienced early childhood losses, dependency disorders, antisocial behavior, or excessive neuroticism, grief will be a more difficult process. Because grief is a stressor of high proportions, these individuals will need extra help in getting through their loss.

HOW DO WE GET THROUGH BEREAVEMENT?

When I asked the participants in the Tampa Study how they managed to survive their grief, they gave me an unequivocal answer: "My family and friends." They said that these were the people who held them up and gave them the strength to finally resolve their grief. They sat with them and shared their tears. They heard their anger and did not run away from it. They nurtured them until they could manage their lives for themselves.

We desperately need the comfort and support of as many people as we can get. Human beings are like herd animals; we don't do well alone under any circumstance. When there is unusual trauma, such as a significant loss, we especially need others near us.

Needing to Feel Secure

Our need for security relates directly to our need for safety. Bereaved people recognize that they have an immense need for safety and that this is not a safe time. The anxiety of early grief has its roots in the incredible fear we experience when our world suddenly explodes before our eyes. Because of our vulnerability and insecurity during early grief, the death throws us back into an earlier level of functioning. We feel like lost children, awkward and self-conscious. We have a tremendous need to lean on other people for basic comfort. At the same time, our reactions feel too much like a conscious regression into childhood, when we had little control over ourselves. As a result, we will often try to hide our fears from others, hoping to control the situation ourselves. Our problem is that we won't be able to ventilate our feelings or work through our grief if we don't feel a small amount of security with another person.

Opening Ourselves to the Pain

There is no avoiding the pain of grief. If we try to distract ourselves by plunging into other things, sooner or later we will be reminded that the pain is still there waiting for us. Hurtful, angry, or guilty feelings that we try to deny stay with us for years. By resisting them, we merely delay the onset of grief and stretch out the process of bereavement. It is far better to deal with our painful memories as soon as we can, and free ourselves of the sadness of grief. For some of us, hanging on to painful memories is a way to not forget our beloved person; at least we have those memories and we know how they feel. We fear that, by resolving the grief, we will lose all the memories that were so precious. This fear is far from the truth. What happens, instead, is that we are able to gain a new perspective about the person's life and find meaning in our own as well.

Accepting Appropriate Grief

When we do our grief work, we are able to arrive at a different place with our memories. Those memories will always be bittersweet and terribly poignant. Grief work helps us to remember the loved one appropriately, to see and focus on the good times rather than the recent past, which was dominated by the death and loss. When we take that view, we begin to see the meaning of the person's life.

Understanding Grief

To learn more about the grieving process is probably the most important focus we can have after a significant loss. Because we know so little about bereavement, we are poorly prepared to deal with it when it happens. Studies have shown that people cope better when they are armed with appropriate information and expectations. There is a cultural need to educate people about the process of bereavement. If we know in advance what is coming next, we are less afraid and better able to feel some semblance of control. One of the greatest problems in helping grieving people is their resistance to moving forward; they fear what is coming next. A better understanding of the process would alleviate that concern.

WILL IT EVER END?

In psychotherapy or when I am lecturing, this is the question I encounter most often, concerning grief and loss. Predicting how long it will take to complete the process of bereavement is difficult. All the variables that I outlined earlier—ambivalence, how death occurred, or who died—will make a difference. Some individuals can complete the entire process in a month; others may take years. Much depends on the relationship we have had with the person who died, the coping skills we may possess, and the degree of shock produced at the time of death. Given these qualifications, it is easy to see why we have difficulty setting time limitations for when we should be finished with our grieving. We simply do not know.

The passage of time can allow us to adapt to the changes taking place, to process our feelings, and to take care of the secondary losses, such as financial instability, that occur after a death. If we had to do everything in a hurry, we would be more overwhelmed than we already are.

Hope

The hope of grief lies in our ability to grow. Many lessons present themselves throughout the grieving process. At a time when we couldn't care less about growing, we are given countless opportunities to do just that. When we are torn from a most significant relationship, we are presented with the possibility of learning more about compassion and love.

Jennifer is a particularly poignant example of hopelessness turning to hope and growth through bereavement. She had been married to Tom for five years. They were both young; she was twenty-nine, he was thirty-one. They had one little girl, three years old, and Jennifer was expecting her next child in two months. Tom, a young engineer just starting out, was not making enough money to support a family of four. He worked extra hours on a second job.

One night, he stopped at a convenience store around 11:00 P.M. That was the last time anyone saw him alive. He was found several feet from the store around midnight, shot in the head. Apparently, he had been held up, had tried to run after his assailant, and was killed in the attempt.

When I first saw Jennifer, she was grief-stricken. Yet, even with all she had lost, she maintained a spiritual tranquillity. She talked of Tom, telling me how much she had learned from him during their marriage, how deeply spiritual he was. She said, "Tom always had a strong faith in God and always believed that we were being watched over. No matter what happened to us, even something bad, he would say it was God's way of teaching us an important lesson. He truly believed that. And I came to believe it, too. If I allow myself even a moment of doubt now, I think I would be betraying what Tom stood for. It is up to me to keep going and take care of our children the way he would want me to do."

I followed Jennifer through the birth of her second little girl and she never faltered in her belief. Six months after delivering her daughter, she enrolled in the university to complete her business degree. Fortunately, her parents helped her with the children.

The last time I met with her, she told me of her new feelings about herself. "If anyone would have told me a few years ago what was going to happen to our family, I would have been horrified. I'm still horrified. But going through it one step at a time gave me the strength to do it. Every time I tried to look ahead and started worrying, I would stop myself. I would remind myself that God was watching over me and that there was a plan in this situation that was going to bring some good. I am a much stronger person than I was when Tom was alive. I guess I relied on him all the time. When he left, I knew it was up to me to take over for him—and me. It hasn't been easy, but it has worked."

There is a way through grief. It isn't easy, but it works. In the end, we become stronger people, more competent at taking care of ourselves, more compassionate at taking care of others.

The Phases of Grief

The process of grief is not a linear progression. By that I mean that we do not move upward through our grief in a steady climb, like the slanting lines that show a good day on the stock market. That would be too easy. Instead, our process is much more jagged, rising on occasion when we feel better, and then falling back and regressing on our awful days. We often hit a cul-de-sac where we remain for a time before we continue our slow climb out of the abyss of our grief toward resolution and renewal.

In my bereavement research, I discovered that an individual passes through five distinct phases in the process of bereavement: shock, awareness of loss, conservation/withdrawal, healing, and renewal. The phases do not have clear-cut stopping and starting points. The process is free-flowing: symptoms of one phase often overlap those of the next phase. We can often get stuck in one phase or another and stay there for a while.

Sometimes, we may be moving well into the next phase when something—a sudden memory, a crisis, a new fear—causes us to regress for a time to the previous phase. When this happens, there is a danger that we'll believe we are going nowhere except crazy. This is quite normal and should be expected. Nothing proceeds perfectly. With patience, we can accept that, in time, this particular rough spot will pass. We don't have to go back to the beginning to begin again.

The bereavement phases are described in the next five chapters. You may find that you are experiencing some of the symptoms of a particular phase but not all of them. Again, this is quite normal; each person doesn't usually experience all the symptoms of grief anyhow. You will generally recognize enough of them to be able to determine what phase you are currently in. Knowing where you are in the grief process will allow you to be more knowledgeable and less afraid of what is to come.

Remember one important thing about grief: YOU WILL FEEL BETTER EVENTUALLY. Unfortunately, grief takes a long time and requires patience. Symptoms and intensities of grief will vary in each person. We don't grieve alike because no person is exactly like another. But, if we keep trying, we will all reach renewal—changed, improved, and wiser.

2

The First Phase: Shock

I thought I was ready. We have never had much death in my family, and I guess I didn't know what to expect. But I really thought I was ready—until it happened and I had to walk out of that hospital alone for the last time. I guess it hit me then. I would never see him again. And I must have gone into shock because I felt sort of numb for a long time after that.

Adult son, age 48

There is little question that the first reaction to a major loss is shock. Whether a death is anticipated or happens suddenly and unexpectedly, we all feel some degree of shock and disbelief. None of us is prepared for the stillness of death. I remember one woman whose father had been in a coma for three months. The year before, he had had a stroke that left him paralyzed and helpless. The family rallied together to see that he received the best medical attention. They transferred him to Johns Hopkins Hospital for treatment. At first, he responded well. The family was elated. Then, after a few weeks, he began to lose ground and the reality became evident. He would not recover. There was nothing more the doctors could do. His family took him back to his hometown hospital where, shortly afterward, he went into a coma. Even then, the family still hoped that a miracle would occur.

How could this strong, capable man get weaker and even perhaps die? His death seemed impossible. They stayed with him in his hospital room throughout the last three months, each adult family member taking a turn. Realizing that there was no real hope, they still felt, in their loyalty, that they should be near him, in case he should come out of the coma even for a minute. He died on a Sunday evening around 6 P.M. His daughter told me that the whole family was gathered around his bed when he died.

She described how her family moved about during the rituals as if they were in a trance. Actually, they were in a state of shock, unable to imagine how life would be without him. Even after their long preparation, they were filled with disbelief that he could be gone from them.

Why is it so hard for us to accept the finality of death? We do not willingly let go of a dearly loved person even when death is close and inevitable. It is almost impossible for us to accept that our world has changed so suddenly. Overnight, we are required to alter our perceptions and redirect our focus to deal with a world that is radically different and empty.

Shock is a general term used to describe the amount of trauma we sustain. Naturally, the amount of trauma will depend on many things: how the death occurred, when or where it happened, or even how it happened. If the death described above had been quick and accidental, the shock experienced by the family members would probably have been even more severe. It is important to keep in mind that the conditions in which the death occurs affect the severity and length of the shock phase. Beyond the initial trauma, how we deal with shock and how we let others help us through this first phase of bereavement will determine the entire course of our grief. We will need a tremendous amount of support during this initial phase. We need to be almost physically held up, just to have the strength to get through the rituals of death.

It is important to remember that we will deal with shock in very individualized ways. We may be numb and unresponding. We may scream, faint, rant, or rave. We may act as if nothing different has happened. For the most part, we will respond to shock in much the same way as we have responded to other severe stressors in our life. Our reactions, whatever they may be, are normal in that they are usually quite typical of our general behavior. *Grief doesn't change us, but it exaggerates our usual response patterns.*

CHARACTERISTICS OF THE SHOCK PHASE

The shock phase of grief has several general characteristics. We may not experience all of them, but there is evidence that most people experience a good number of them. They have been identified as:

- State of alarm
- Disbelief
- Confusion
- Restlessness
- Feelings of unreality
- Helplessness.

State of Alarm

When we are in shock, our bodies are in a state of severe physiological alarm. This physical response is a natural reaction when our sense of security is threatened. We do not perceive the world as safe any longer, so we set up a defensive reaction that keeps us alert to anything that is unusual or fearful.

The alarm response is controlled by the sympathetic part of the autonomic nervous system. When mobilized, this system acts to move blood away from our hands and feet, causing icy fingers, sweaty palms, and even, sometimes, trembling in our entire body. Blood is moved away from the gastrointestinal tract, cutting our appetite and often causing nausea. Excessive quantities of hormones are pumped through the bloodstream, helping to mobilize us for action.

We experience a fear response that energizes us to react to a threat of danger. C. S. Lewis described this accurately in his book *A Grief Observed:* "No one ever told me that grief felt so like fear. I am not afraid, but the sensation is like being afraid. The same fluttering in the stomach, the same restlessness, the yawning. I keep on swallowing." When we experience a severe loss, the reactions feel very much like fear and sometimes close to panic; consequently, our bodies set up a defensive position to protect ourselves.

Disbelief

Disbelief and denial actually help us in bereavement because they act as buffers. They allow us to process the reality of the loss gradually. Without this protection, the pain of grief would be too intense to bear. We would be completely overwhelmed. In early grief, it is almost impossible to think of anything but the loss. Denial and disbelief offer short, temporary retreats from the awful reality of the death. We gain a brief respite that allows us to endure again the awful, agonizing pain.

Confusion

Many bereaved people, particularly in the early days of their grief, tell me they are worried about their lingering confused state of mind. They can't remember to do things, they have a hard time concentrating, they lose things like keys, eyeglasses, or checkbooks, and they find it almost impossible to make decisions. I assure them that these reactions are absolutely normal and will eventually pass. Our world is shattered when a loved one is taken from us. Our emotions are on a roller coaster, and the next fearful plunge may send us into despair. What had been constant and dependable before is no longer available to us. Our habitual patterns are broken. We can no longer rely on the world as we have known it.

Accordingly, we must invent new patterns of responding. Each step or decision requires attention that, until then, was handled in a habitual manner. The overload of new information confuses us. One young bereaved mother said her mind felt like a computer gone haywire.

Restlessness

Our restless behavior in early bereavement seems like a paradox. Just when we feel frozen and need to sit down and rest, we find instead that we are driven to keep moving—an indication of the state of alarm we are experiencing. Increased muscle tension, brought about by the activation of the sympathetic nervous system, causes us to pace, fidget, and move aimlessly about from room to room. We may start to go into another room to get something, only to forget what it was that we wanted. It always seems strange to me that our culture offers so little to the bereaved to help them burn off some of their restlessness. Because everything is done for us, we have little choice but to sit quietly by, our hands folded in our laps, allowing others to take over various tasks, while our bodies' systems and our minds seem to be racing at breakneck speed.

Feelings of Unreality

During this first phase of bereavement, we feel that we are moving through an unreal world. Everything has a hazy vagueness; everything looks dim, literally. In the dimness, we must go through the rituals of death, which are foreign to most of us. We have a hard time visualizing ourselves participating in a funeral much less being the leading mourner. Many people have told me that they felt they were standing aside, watching themselves go through the motions of living. One young widow explained it this way:

> It was so strange. I was putting on my makeup, combing my hair, and all the time it was as if I were standing by the door watching myself go through these motions. How else could I have done these things? It was impossible. I was only 38 and I was getting ready to go to my husband's funeral.

This psychological distancing is a defense we all use when we are faced with an emotionally painful situation. Psychic numbing lets us temporarily remove ourselves from the painful event until we are better able to deal with it.

Helplessness

Death causes us to feel helpless. It is one of the events of life over which we have little control. Nothing can be done to bring back our beloved person. The sheer frustration of our loss taunts us. We feel out of control; our world has become unsafe, unpredictable. We are like children again, in a world of grown-ups. We feel the same awful helplessness we did when we had little or no control over our childhood world.

After my son was killed, I used to go back over every minute of the accident, trying to identify one event that could have made things turn out differently. "If I had not let him use the boat," or "If only we had gone to the beach instead of staying home." My helplessness at not being able to change the course of events lingered for years after his death.

One young bereaved mother in my Tampa Study described her feelings of helplessness this way:

> We don't have a lot of things to worry about. We know we don't have any regrets of our relationship with our son because everything was so beautiful that we don't have that to worry about. And we don't have any financial problems, you know, hanging over us from his sickness and all that,

or, as a mater of fact, any problems at all. It's just the fact
that life seems so hopeless now that all of our dreams are
just shattered.

PHYSICAL SYMPTOMS
OF THE SHOCK PHASE

Grief is a multilayered phenomenon. We feel it on many
levels at once. We used to think of grief only in emotional
terms, but research has shown that physical and social aspects play equally important roles. We experience a variety
of physical symptoms during the shock phase of grief. They
include:

◆ Dry mouth
◆ Sighing or yawning
◆ Generalized weakness
◆ Crying
◆ Trembling
◆ Startle response
◆ Inability to sleep
◆ Poor appetite.

Sometimes, a heaviness in our bodies makes us feel that we
are made of lead. One moment, we want to just sit and stare,
only to be forced by some inner urging to get up and move
about again.

We often experience a startle response, especially following an accidental death. Every time I would think of the
boat crashing into my son's body after his accident, my own
body would jerk as if I were receiving the impact myself.

Two important symptoms of this phase are poor appetite
and sleeping difficulties. Both of these symptoms are in-
dicative of the tremendous trauma and generalized stress
that we go through in early bereavement. We feel nauseated
much of the time because blood is moved away from our
stomachs. Our bodies reel from the force of grief.

SOCIAL ASPECTS OF THE SHOCK PHASE

Each person will experience individual social effects of a death, depending on his or her relationships in the community and in a close circle of friends. These are the social aspects that are common to all of us:

◆ Turning inward
◆ Preoccupation with thoughts of the lost person
◆ Rituals of death.

Turning Inward

When our world has become unsafe, chaotic, and empty, we turn inward to ourselves for protection. We lose interest in newspapers or television or friends around us, and prefer to focus on our roller-coaster thoughts. We feel severed from the real world. All our thoughts are on the one who is gone. C. S. Lewis, in *A Grief Observed,* wrote after the death of his wife:

> There is a sort of invisible blanket between the world and me. I find it hard to take in what anyone says. Or perhaps hard to want to take it in. It is so uninteresting. Yet I want others to be about me. I dread the moments when the house is empty. If only they would talk to one another and not to me.

Preoccupation with Thoughts of the Lost Person

"She is constantly on my mind" or "Thoughts of him never leave me." Such statements are typical of the first phase of grief, and continue into the second and third phases. A woman who attended a seminar where I spoke told me:

> Sometimes I think I'm going out of my mind with thoughts of Bill. I see him in the hospital, when he came out of

surgery. Worse yet, I see him when he died hooked up to those tubes and machines. It's awful. I can't block out those pictures. It is as if we had no life, no memories before the cancer.

Try as we might, in this early phase of grief we can't blot out the grim inner pictures. These death-related thoughts and images continue with relentless drive. How did it ever happen? Why did it happen? How could it have been stopped? What went on just before the death? Our minds grow weary of trying to figure things out when there are no real answers.

Rituals of Death

The rituals of death require a lot from us, not the least of which is that first awful, wrenching trip to the funeral home to make the arrangements. Those of us who make arrangements ahead of time do ourselves and our survivors a great favor. Without prearrangements, we are faced with many decisions that must be made at a time when we are least prepared to make them. What type of funeral? What type of casket? How should the person be clothed? These questions bombard us and, if we aren't ready with answers (who ever is?), we will feel overwhelmed.

For some of us, the second visit to the funeral home, to view our beloved family member, may be even harder. Getting the nerve to walk up to the casket can be frightening. We don't know what to expect. If we're lucky, we gain a sense of peace when we see how serene the deceased can look. An adult daughter said of her mother:

> I didn't know what to expect, you know. Mom had been sick for a long time and had gotten so thin. She had lost most of her hair and the wig we got for her never looked good on her. It just looked strange after always seeing her with a bun. I didn't know what to expect. So I really hung

back and let my older sister and her husband go first. It was really scary in a way, not knowing what to expect. But when I saw her, I was relieved. She looked peaceful and even had a touch of a smile on her face. The way they had fixed her up made her look like she was just sleeping. I thought I could even see her breathing, but I knew that couldn't be true. So I felt a little better after that.

Getting through a funeral takes courage. Friends and family members help, but we are still in shock. We still use a buffer of disbelief and vagueness to help us get through this raw phase of grief.

At least the funeral provides us with a socially acceptable place to grieve. The problem for most of us is that we are too embarrassed to show our grief. We struggle to keep the lump in our throat down or to hide the chest convulsions that come with gut-wrenching tears. We would do ourselves a service if we could allow our grief to take whatever direction it needs, without putting a clamp on our feelings.

Medical researchers warn that stifling emotions such as crying, anger, or feelings of guilt can be detrimental to our emotional and physical health. The high death and illness rates among bereaved people attest to this danger.

The shock phase, for all its confusion, helps us adapt by forming an insulation against the chaotic outside world. Shock dulls and numbs much of our suffering until we can better deal with it, until we can process the actuality of death.

As impossibly painful as this phase is for most of us, we somehow manage to get through it. Shock can last anywhere from a few minutes to several weeks. However, it usually passes into the next phase of grief when the funeral is over and the emotions that have been held in too tightly begin to overflow. We become aware of the loneliness of grief when friends and family move back into their daily lives and we are left alone. At this time, a variety of emotions erupt, often with the force of a major volcano. The second phase of grief has begun.

ENDING THE SHOCK PHASE

How to Help Yourself

◆ Recognize that you have an immense need for safety and that this is not a safe time. The anxiety of early grief is based on the incredible fear we experience at having our world suddenly explode before our eyes. Try to find safety in small ways, such as having a close friend or family member stay with you.

◆ Don't feel you have to be brave. Holding in emotions takes much more energy than releasing them. Individuals who are involved with their grief and are guided through it will adapt better than those who don't acknowledge their grief.

◆ Allow others to nurture you. In this phase of grief, you are beset with anxiety and helplessness. Your thoughts are not as coherent as they are normally. Consequently, this is a time when you need to lean on others both physically and emotionally.

◆ If you aren't receiving the nurturance you want or need, ask for it. Often, supporters are afraid to be too forward, fearing you are especially fragile. They might need some encouragement. The important thing is that you get the support and care that you need.

◆ Be patient with yourself. You will feel confused, you will feel restless and agitated, and you will probably lose things. Allow yourself the leeway to experience whatever you do without self-chastisement. Your conduct may not be the way you normally behave, but it is all a part of the natural process of bereavement.

◆ Don't worry that you still refer to the deceased as if the death had not occurred. He or she is still in your heart. You are still very much oriented to your lost loved person. You know in your head what has happened, but it will take some time to fully know it in your heart.

◆ Take an active part in the funeral planning, if you can. Having a say in what happens—such as asking friends or family members to give eulogies, designating favorite readings that might be included, or selecting desired music—is an important element of the ritual. Providing input gives a feeling of being in some control, in an otherwise out-of-control situation. Besides, later you will be proud that you were able to contribute to this important function.

◆ Make no major decisions about your future life. It is impossible for you to gather your wits about you immediately after the death. Give yourself time to decide.

3

The Second Phase: Awareness of Loss

I was in my office, seated on the couch across from a
new patient whose husband had died in a tragic car accident only three months before. An attractive woman of
54, her face showed the agony of recent grief. "How long
is this awful pain going to last?" she asked. "I thought I
was doing OK in the beginning. I was able to take care of
all the arrangements. I even consoled my family and
friends. What has happened to me? I'm a wreck. I can't
stop crying."

The second phase of grief—
awareness of loss—is marked by strong emotions that seesaw haphazardly through each day. We may wake up feeling
anxious, afraid to get out of bed. Or, we may start the day
calmly, only to find that later we are wracked with spasms
of pain and uncontrollable weeping.

During the initial phase of grief, shock provides a temporary buffer against the emotional turmoil of loss. When we
enter the second phase, that insulation is stripped away and
we are left feeling raw and exposed.

CHARACTERISTICS OF THE
AWARENESS-OF-LOSS PHASE

◆ Separation anxiety
◆ Conflicts

◆ Acting out emotional expectations
◆ Prolonged stress

Separation Anxiety

When an emotional bond is broken forever, the pain is akin
to having an arm or a leg torn away from our bodies. At a
psychic level, this is exactly what has happened. Our emotional investment in someone we love is deeply entrenched.
For most of us, an interdependence with that person is established at a deep psychological level. After the bond is
severed, the raw stump is painfully exposed. This awareness-
of-loss phase is marked by acute emotional disorganization.
Much of the time, we fear that we are on the edge of a nervous breakdown.

Our safety has been radically uprooted by the loss. The
things we had come to expect and depend on in our world
are no longer available. We are left feeling vulnerable and
frightened, like abandoned children. Separation anxiety
produces a feeling of danger, of unsafeness, and we struggle
for some control over our chaotic world. Separation anxiety
often makes us feel that a quick replacement will ease our
grief. But if we haven't done our grief work, the replacement
will only be a temporary distraction.

Warren Brown had been married 45 years to a woman
who was a cohort and companion. They were both artists,
and they taught and worked together all their married life.
Warren told me that theirs wasn't a marriage in which the
husband went off to work and came home only to eat dinner and watch TV. "We were together all the time and
shared a tremendously close marriage." On the morning of
her sixty-third birthday, Mrs. Brown accidentally drowned
in their swimming pool. Warren had gone to a florist, to
pick up the traditional red roses he always gave her on
special occasions. He was gone not more than thirty minutes. Returning, he found her lifeless body floating in the

pool. All his efforts to revive her failed. She had been underwater too long. Apparently, she had slipped on the side of the pool, was knocked unconscious, and fell into the pool and drowned.

The next few days were a nightmare. Warren was unable to realize what had happened. After the funeral, his neighbors and friends included him in invitations to dinners and, after a while, to parties. At one of the parties a few weeks later, Warren met a woman whom he liked very much. She was empathic and listened quietly as he talked of the drowning. They began dating. Yet, all the while, Warren had no hesitation in describing the woman as his "substitute." He found her to be, in many ways, like his wife. He was trying to replace his wife as quickly as he could and avoid the pain of separation.

Even with the comfort offered by a new companion, Warren was unable to part with his wife's things (it would have meant parting with her). Her cosmetics were still on their shelves in the bathroom; all her clothes and personal items were just as she had left them. During the time when Warren needed to be releasing his dead wife in order to move on with his life, he tried instead to pretend she hadn't died. He even pretended that, by finding a quick substitute, he could continue his life as if nothing were changed.

Unfortunately, separation anxiety must be worked through before we attach to another. Unless we have experienced the pain of loss and dealt with our fears of abandonment, we will remain in a state of suspended animation. We will be unable to grow through the loss, unable to rely on and love ourselves, and, consequently, unable to fully love another person.

Slowly, over the next year, Warren's health began to deteriorate. His interest in his new relationship began to falter. Two years later, he suffered a fatal heart attack. Apparently, he had pushed himself too fast and too hard. Avoiding the work of grief took more energy than he had realized. Warren simply burned out.

Conflicts

Loss seems to bring on a multitude of conflicts. They sweep over us when we are least able to resolve them. Several of the widows in the Tampa Study were afraid to live alone but hesitated to live with someone else. Barbara, a fifty-eight-year-old widow, invited both of her children and their families to move in with her. She was terrified of living by herself. Yet, when the two families finally moved into her small home, she was a nervous wreck from the noise and congestion caused by eight extra people. By then, she did not know how to ask them to move or even whether she wanted them to. Another widow, who had few friends in Tampa, wanted to make a trip to visit close friends. But the attention needed by her three dogs, two cats, and canary kept her near her home most of the time. She rarely had a visitor and was extremely lonely. She wondered how she would ever make new friends when she had to stay so close to home. Yet she couldn't face the loss of her beloved pets so soon after the loss of her husband.

Our conflicts are especially difficult in bereavement because they usually present other losses—things that are too painful to accept when the hurt is already intolerable. *My advice is to keep life as simple as possible.* You will probably experience conflicts. When you do, either try to put them off or try to resolve them quickly.

Acting Out Emotional Expectations

One Saturday morning, when I was living in Tampa, I opened my mail and discovered some wonderful news. I immediately rushed to the phone to call Mother and tell her. My hand was already on the receiver when I realized, with an awful pang of disappointment and grief, that Mother was no longer alive. She had been gone only three or four weeks. I remember standing there sobbing my heart out.

Emotional acceptance of death is slow to arrive. For example, a widow sets her husband's place at the table before realizing that he is no longer there. A bereaved father starts to go into a sporting goods store to check on some new baseball equipment; then he remembers his son is no longer there to use it. A widower remembers a beautiful sunset the day before, and begins to describe it. Then he realizes that his wife is no longer there to hear. Mr. Black, an elderly widower, told me that he worked in his wife's garden after her death, trying to keep it up as meticulously as she had. Sometimes, he said, he would come upon an unexpected and beautiful bud and would find himself calling out to her in sudden excitement before he realized she was not there. The awareness of death, the reality of separation, continues to produce a raw pain as each expectation is met with frustration and disappointment.

Prolonged Stress

There is no question that grief uses enormous quantities of psychic energy. This expenditure, in turn, causes us debilitating stress. Simply surviving each day saps our strength and leaves us open to possible illness or even to accidents. A great deal of evidence connects long-lasting stress to a breakdown of the immune system, which invites many infectious diseases.

Physical stress, however, is not the main problem in our expenditure of energy. The seesaw effect of emotional outbursts during this phase creates the largest drain on our energy supply. It is impossible to tell when we will collapse into doubled-up spasms of pain. Anything can trigger this response—suddenly hearing a song that was special to us both, or uncovering a photograph or personal item that we didn't expect to find.

It takes a lot of energy to cry or to feel rage, guilt, or frustration—sometimes all at once. Nevertheless, it takes more energy to hold back these emotional outbursts.

For this reason, releasing pent-up emotions is far healthier than holding them in. In the long run, it is better to give in to our feelings and ride out this turbulent period of painful grief.

SYMPTOMS OF THE AWARENESS-OF-LOSS PHASE

◆ Yearning
◆ Frustration
◆ Crying
◆ Anger
◆ Guilt
◆ Shame
◆ Sleep disturbance
◆ Fear of death

We will not necessarily feel all these symptoms, and we might experience other unique symptoms that are not listed here. This phase of emotional upheaval involves many different responses, and the sheer number of outbursts overwhelms us. One, or even two, can be managed by most people; when five or ten emotional explosions take place within an hour, it becomes impossible to cope with anything else.

Yearning

Our longing to have our loved ones with us is intensified when we face the awareness that they are no longer here. A middle-aged widow said to me, "I can't understand why I have actual pain in my chest when I feel particularly lonely. It's at times like these when I long for him to be here to hold me and talk to me. The feeling is so intense that I want to scream or beat on something. And I can't do a thing about it." Yearning is an attempt to recover our loved one. The child in us is resisting abandonment and seeking reassurance.

Mrs. Reiner had lived with her husband on a farm for all their married years. When he died, she found it comforting to put on one of her husband's old plaid shirts. She said it made her feel as though his arms were around her. Others have told me that they had saved a favorite piece of clothing and just took it out of a box or drawer and held it from time to time. These personal belongings bring comfort when we have a deep need to make some sort of contact. Our need is a form of searching. The comfort offered by these belongings is a form of finding our lost one and feeling a sense of closeness once again.

Frustration

Frustration is a direct result of yearning and *not* finding. When death has deprived us forever of a beloved person who has been an integral part of our lives, we feel tremendous frustration. We desperately want to find them again, and our continuous, unsatisfied yearning traps us in constant unresolved frustration. One widow said:

> I go to work in the morning and during the day my mind is fairly well occupied, and I forget that he is gone. When I come home at night, I rush into the house expecting to find John. It is not until I turn on the hall light that I remember he is not here. Then I die inside all over again. When will I get used to his being gone?

Our frustration reminds us that we are still children at heart, when it comes to our fears of being abandoned. Our pain is reminiscent of when we were left by our parents; we were alone, isolated, and frightened. The frustration we experience translates to irritation much of the time, and that attitude becomes a normal part of the bereavement process.

Crying

It is hard to know in advance just what will trigger our tears, but crying always seems to occur in waves. One widow described her feelings this way:

> I don't know what happened to me that whole year. I'd go to church and I'd be sitting next to a girl and she's liable to say, How are you today? or just anything. And . . . the tears would just flood. And I couldn't stop them, ... It was like that for a whole year.

Some of us find it difficult to cry in front of others. We consider crying a sign of weakness and we feel humiliated. We reserve it for times when we are alone. One widow in the Tampa Study wouldn't even let her children see her cry. She felt she should be strong in front of everyone. But, she added, "There are times when I cry all night long."

In the middle of seemingly endless tears, it's important to remember that crying can help us adapt to loss. It offers a healthy and much needed release for pent-up emotions. It's the steam release on our inner tea kettle, and it keeps us from exploding inside or out. Crying alerts others to our need for help and support, and this need shouldn't be underestimated. Most of the people who have described their grief to me have told me of the value of an active support system. They could call their friends and know that help would be there when they needed it. Some people have said that, without their friends, they wouldn't have made it through their mourning.

Anger

Anger is a natural part of grief, a constant companion of frustration, helplessness, and deprivation. We may not consciously acknowledge our anger, but it is usually there to some degree. I have found that there are six sources of anger that cause us major despair and discomfort when we are grieving: confrontive anger, displaced anger, ambivalent anger, internalized anger, helpless anger, and appropriate anger.

Confrontive Anger

When we don't get the support and encouragement we need from our family and friends, we feel isolated, betrayed, or deserted. We react by confronting our family with irritability and hostility rather than simply asking for more support.

Displaced Anger

Sometimes we misdirect our anger toward persons who are not responsible for the death but who happen to be handy— the hospital staff, the funeral director, the minister, or God. We desperately need to blame *someone* for this horrible tragedy that has hurt us so deeply. We sometimes get angry with the person who has died, for not taking appropriate health or safety precautions, abandoning us, or causing us immediate hardship. All of these thoughts are quite normal and understandable. They allow us to have a scapegoat when there is no one else to blame. This transferred anger will pass when we can accept the death a little better.

Ambivalent Anger

No relationship is perfect. We can all remember times when we were upset with our spouses, children, parents, and friends. This unevenness is normal and natural, but, when we are going through a major loss, these memories often assault us. After each loss I experienced, angrily spoken words that I thought I had forgotten long ago would slip back from some part of my mind and I would feel guilty. If we think we must be *perfectly* loving in our relationships and in our memories during our bereavement, we put ourselves under enormous strain and deny the outlet that healthy anger can provide.

Internalized Anger

Anger is considered antisocial in our culture, especially among women. Rather than show our anger, we sometimes turn it inward. When anger is turned inward, it can often cause physical problems such as asthma, arthritis, ulcers, or hypertension. Repressed anger has also been connected to nightmares, feelings of hopelessness, and depression. Most importantly, internalized anger blocks the resolution of our grief and prevents us from moving on toward a new life. It is far better for us to direct our anger outward, rather than to turn it toward ourselves.

Helpless Anger

The sheer helplessness of our frustration and deprivation when we must give up a dearly loved person leaves us feeling powerless and out of control. We tend to express this form of anger with tears and agitation rather than with angry outbursts. Again, this is a form of turning our anger inward. Processing our anger with a counselor or trusted friend can help us to regain some feelings of inner control.

Appropriate Anger

When we can express openly our anger at the awful situation we are experiencing, we are dealing with anger in an appropriate way. I recommend screaming, beating a pillow against the bed, and allowing some space—a particular room, an outdoor spot, a time or activity—for expressing painful deprivation and helplessness. This venting of anger can be done alone or with a trusted friend. I have beat plenty of pillows, and it works. It is amazing what relief it can bring, at least for a little while, until another "fix" is needed.

Anger could be seen as appropriate when it is turned toward those who were in some way directly responsible for the death, through negligence or violence. A murder, a manslaughter, or a death caused by an alcoholic driver would be a situation where anger would be appropriate. Venting our anger in a purposeful manner, such as working as a volunteer with Mothers Against Drunk Drivers (MADD) or similar organizations that try to correct these situations, can be healing and helpful at the same time.

Coping with Anger

Anger is a difficult emotion to express in bereavement, because we feel that we are under the close scrutiny of others. We want to do things correctly and set a good example. But *we* are the most important persons during this time, and we need to take care of ourselves, especially now. Our own needs should be our top priority. When we take care of ourselves, we set the best example of all.

Guilt

Unfortunately, guilt seems to be a natural by-product of the grief process. Even when we have been exemplary parents, children, caregivers, or mates and have taken care of everything in the best way possible, we will usually focus on something that we did wrong or did not do at all. There are many basic forms of guilt, but I am mentioning the two forms that I think are the most debilitating: causal guilt and survivor guilt.

Causal Guilt

When my son was killed, I remember feeling guilty about everything. Why didn't I ask him to come home sooner? Why wasn't I nicer to him the week before, when he had made me angry? Why didn't we get contact lenses for him, so that he could see better? (The fact that he couldn't have worn them while water skiing made little difference.) I agonized over every detail, until I was worn out. A widow in the Tampa Study anguished over not sensing that her husband was ill and not being able to detect trouble sooner, even when the symptoms were not observable:

> How would I know if someone never talked? I feel guilty sometimes that maybe if I had looked at him more and had seen that he was looking tired. . . . But he always said he was tired, you know. And working in the station, he was tired. But then I remind myself, surely you could have seen; but I never did stop to think. . . . I really couldn't have, you know. . . . I guess I am really not to blame because he didn't tell me he felt bad.

Guilt comes from a wide variety of sources. Unfortunately, when we carry guilt for a long period of time, it can slow down the bereavement process and keep us stuck in the awareness-of-loss phase. Then, instead of using our energies to heal, we stay churned up with guilt and we waste valuable strength on useless thoughts.

Survivor Guilt

In our culture, death is considered the worst thing that can happen. When someone we love dies, we feel guilty just because we are still alive. I remember that, after Jim's death, I didn't want to eat because he could never eat again. Watching a beautiful sunset seemed selfish, because he would never be able to see one again.

Survivor guilt is particularly strong in parents who have lost a child. We cannot comprehend that we have outlived our child; how can the natural order of the universe have been reversed? From the moment of conception, most parents feel responsible for their children's safety, care, and upbringing. To lose a child seems a personal failure, and it is not easily dealt with. We feel that we somehow neglected to do the job assigned to us.

Guilt leads to feelings of unworthiness, shame, and self-blame. If these feelings continue, the result is a lifetime of misery. The best way to deal with this ugly emotion is to share our feelings with a trusted friend or counselor. If we are to heal, it is important to bring our feelings out into the light, where they can be truly seen. Usually, after a time of acknowledging them, they tend to fade. Guilt reminds me of a slug. It can thrive only in dark, damp places. Lift it out onto a sunny walkway and it shrivels and dies.

Shame

Shame is different from guilt. Guilt says, "You have done something wrong or left undone something that you should have done." Shame says, "You are the mistake. You are the error." Because grief makes us feel alienated and victimized, we seem different from other people. We feel that we are being singled out and punished by some higher court, undeservedly.

Our principles and ideals are established by the teachings and example of our family of origin and the society we live in. We feel comfortable following these principles because they give us a sense of belonging: we are a part of a larger system. No one wants to feel alone. Our personal loss makes us feel alone, different from others, no longer in control of our lives. We see our loss as a penalty, and we are afraid of how society will view us.

One bereaved mother said to me, "I felt as if I were standing on a mountaintop being tossed around by the wind, exposed and vulnerable like the gnarled old trees above the timberline." She said that she felt punished by some cosmic force for a crime against society that she did not commit. The stigma of death, a common burden among survivors, makes us feel alienated and stripped.

Guilt can be removed through confession, but shame can be handled only by finally resolving our grief—regaining a sense of personal control, developing a stronger sense of self and purpose, and reversing the negative view of death as punishment.

Sleep Disturbance

Problems with getting enough sleep still plague us during the awareness-of-loss phase. Sleep is usually fitful and erratic. We're still trying to sort things out and understand what has happened. A young woman whose husband died in a car accident explained:

> I wake up two or three times during the night and stay awake anywhere from thirty minutes to two hours. It isn't that I worry. It's more like I just can't sleep well and I wake up; so naturally, if I wake up, I think . . . till I think myself to sleep again and then I go right back. . . . I wake up and go through the same thing again.

This is a time when we desperately need sleep and, paradoxically, when being able to sleep is most difficult. Everyone advises us to get rest and sleep, but, because we are still using a great deal of energy and burning an oversupply of adrenaline, it is hard for our bodies to relax. We cannot get either enough rest or enough sleep. As to medication, I believe that it is better to take a mild tranquilizer or an antianxiety agent and get some rest than to overextend our physical limits and totally exhaust ourselves. There is no indication that a small amount of medication, prescribed by a physician, slows the grief process or hurts us in any way.

Fear of Death

We seem to be more afraid during bereavement than we ordinarily are. This fear seems really ridiculous: we couldn't care less what happens to us, yet we are fearful that something will. Part of our fear could be a result of feeling closer to death after the loss of a significant person. A part of us seems to have died as well. After Jim died, I remember having to drive across the Tampa Bay Bridge every day and thinking, "It wouldn't bother me if my car went over the edge. At least, I would be out of this awful pain." Yet, I would take extra safety precautions in other things I did. My reaction didn't make a lot of sense to me then. Later, I came to believe that a loss makes us realize, perhaps for the first time, that we are vulnerable to death—it can and will happen to us as well as to others.

PSYCHOLOGICAL ASPECTS OF THE AWARENESS-OF-LOSS PHASE

◆ Oversensitivity
◆ Disbelief and denial
◆ Sensing the deceased's presence
◆ Dreaming

Oversensitivity

We are very sensitive during early bereavement, and we often react to what others say more quickly and negatively than we would at other times. This is hard to get accustomed to, because most of us like to think of ourselves as "good people"—fair, patient, and loving. When we react to family or close friends in any unkind way, we are dismayed with ourselves. Alma's husband had died from lung cancer after a long and painful death. She was exhausted from the constant care she had given him. She told me that she had snapped at nearly everyone, particularly her neighbors. She described one encounter:

> I don't understand why I was so rude to my neighbor when she came over to offer her sympathy. All she said was "I'm sorry," but it flew all over me. In the first place, she didn't even bother to come for a whole week, and, in the second

place, I don't want her feeling sorry for me. But, usually, I'm more easygoing and that wouldn't have ticked me off so.

We shouldn't be hard on ourselves during this phase. We are working intensely, at an unconscious level, to make some sense of an awful tragedy. We are more vulnerable during this time; our wound is still raw and exposed. As we progress through the grief process, we will be able to relax and gain better control of our lives.

Disbelief and Denial

We find it hard to believe something so irreversible as death. We seem possessed by the notion that somehow we will get our beloved back again. We may rationally accept life and death, but, when a severe loss happens, we invent magical ways for our lost person to return. An elderly woman, whose husband had died suddenly of a heart condition, said of this denial:

> I feel worse at times, because it just hits me that it's for good, ... You sort of go through a daze at first, like it's not really happening, or something—I don't know what. But after all this, you get to realize that this is forever, ... And it's not, it's not at all good.

It is perfectly healthy and natural to experience denial from time to time. We can't look at grief all the time; it would be too painful. The ability to step back into the web of disbelief offers us a temporary rest. We can get our bearings for a moment, before plunging back into the rugged work of "letting go."

Sensing the Deceased's Presence

During the awareness-of-loss phase, we seem to feel more acutely the presence of the one who has died. People have described what I term the "flicker phenomenon"—a perception seen at the outside edges of our visual field as a flickering shadow. Immediately, thoughts of the deceased come to mind, but when we look directly at that area, nothing is there. After my mother died, I saw this flickering shadow many times; each time, I felt her presence there. Others have told me of actually seeing the deceased person standing in a doorway or sitting in a favorite chair. Mr. Brown spoke of his experience when he felt his wife's presence:

> I will be washing windows, for example—a job we always did together, one on one side and one on the other—and I will suddenly see her on the other side of the window. Or, I will be sitting here and suddenly look up and she is sitting across from me.

These experiences are not frightening; instead, they seem to bring a sense of comfort to the ones who experience them.

Dreaming

Dreams that seem like visions are not uncommon during bereavement. They generally bring a feeling of calmness to a disquieted mind. In the Tampa Study, one widower told me that, in several dreams, he saw his wife in very ordinary situations around the house. These dreams were soothing; they helped him to feel a little more secure without her. "It was like having her come in occasionally to visit," he said. Another widow talked of feelings a dream had aroused:

> It was not more than a month after George died, I dreamed about him. He was wearing that same old brown leather jacket that he loved so well. I remember him walking through the front door with a big smile telling me that he had quit that old hateful job he had. He really seemed happy. Then I woke and it took a minute for me to realize that he wasn't here. I couldn't help crying . . . because he was finally happy but mostly I cried because I missed him so much.

Mr. and Mrs. Jonas had been married for fifty-two years when he became ill with pneumonia. Because he had emphysema, special precautions were taken and he had around-the-clock nursing care. Nevertheless, he became weaker and weaker, and finally slipped away. Mrs. Jonas had several experiences in which she actually saw her husband in the house. On one occasion, he spoke, but she did not know to whom he was speaking. She described her experience as follows:

> You know, the other morning I got up and I could see him so plain, so plain, and I wondered, maybe I dreamt about him and didn't remember dreaming because . . . he was so plain, like he was around me, you know. I saw him so plain in my mind . . . not a vision. . . . I said, well good heavens, he's gone . . . I'm well aware that he's gone . . . but he looked so good, like he was for real, you know. It seemed like he was trying to say something . . . what in the world was it . . . something like . . . it seemed like I want to go someplace and I don't want to go alone, and he says . . . well, you don't have to go by yourself . . . I'll go with you. Something like that.

Many of the dreams that people in the Tampa Study related to me were dreams of premonition. Several people told me that, for them, dreams of this type had been a lifelong experience. A widow explained these phenomena:

> I have a lot of dreams that are sometimes scary. If I have a dream about something, and it strikes me as being something different and I tell it to my husband or . . . to my children, it really happens. Like, this is one I dreamed: My husband had been married before, and . . . I didn't know him until nine years after they were divorced; but his wife was living—he had two children, like I did, when I married him. And I got up one morning and I told my husband, "You know, maybe I shouldn't say this, but I dreamed of Jane last night." And I told him how she died. And two days later, I was on the phone talking with my stepdaughter, and emergency broke in and said that they wanted to

use the phone and I got off. And she called me right afterwards and told me that her mother had died.

This same woman also dreamed of her husband before he died.

I said to my daughter, "Well, I really shouldn't tell you this, but I dreamed of your Daddy last night. We were both standing real still, side by side, but were naked." And he died two days later. The same thing happens every time I dream of someone. I wish I'd written them all down.

During the awareness-of-loss phase, dreams seem to be most prolific. These "visitations," as they are often called, seem to provide an opportunity for the lost person to say good-bye.

ENDING THE AWARENESS-OF-LOSS PHASE

There is a limit to the amount of emotional outpouring that we can endure until sheer exhaustion forces us to slow down. This exhaustion actually initiates the third phase of bereavement: we need to pull back from others and conserve our precious energy. This shift doesn't occur overnight. We may sense a slowing down for some time, but we still keep on with heavy emotional output and activity. Gradually, enormous fatigue forces us to begin a progressive winddown that moves us into the next phase.

Our main tasks during the awareness-of-loss phase are to experience the pain and not to block off feelings of sorrow, anger, or guilt. It is important not to close off the awareness of loss, even though it might seem easier at the moment to deny the pain that it brings.

Use these actions to work through this phase:

◆ Realize that the pain of loss must be experienced. There is no escape from it.

◆ Expect support to begin to dwindle during this period. People resume their own schedules and go about their own business. They haven't forgotten you, but their busy lives leave little time for prolonged crises.

◆ Don't try to hide your feelings. Allowing others to share your grief will bring continued support.

◆ Give yourself permission to cry. Crying is one of the best ways to reduce pent-up tension. Cry whenever tears well up. Tempestuous, wracking bouts will drain you but will make you feel better in the long run.

◆ Vent your anger. You have a right to be angry. You are frustrated, deprived, and alone. Recognize that anger is a real and normal emotion that wells up in full fury during grief. You may notice that you are more irritable now than at other times in your life. Don't be hard on yourself. It is all a part of grief—the emotional turmoil caused by loss, deprivation, conflict, and confusion.

◆ Talk about your feelings of guilt with someone you trust. Chances are, what you feel guilty about will have been experienced by others. Share it, and you won't feel that you are the only person in the world who has experienced that kind of reaction.

◆ Open up your feelings of shame. Like guilt, shame starts to shrink when it is aired. Shame may be harder to talk about because it hits at our inner core. Work with yourself to express these feelings to a trusted friend.

◆ Talk about your loss, over and over; this repetition is tremendously important during grief. You will be thinking about little else anyhow, so indulge yourself in this way. Do the right thing for yourself by expressing your ruminations.

Because this is the healthiest way toward recognizing and eventually accepting your loss, you will actually be shortening this phase of grief.

◆ Recognize that you are more sensitive during bereavement than at other times. Don't let another person's remark or unsympathetic action throw you into a tailspin or work to alienate you from others when you need them most.

◆ Thank your friends in little ways, for staying with you. They need to know that you appreciate their being there. Pick up an African violet plant, a bottle of wine, a book of verse, or a greeting card. Support is a two-way street, and your effort to think of others will help to lift your spirits a little.

◆ Exercise. Your body is pumping extra adrenaline into your system and needs an outlet. Watch that you don't overdo. Physical workouts help to relieve tension when pent-up emotions can't be released. However, your body is fragile right now, and you are using all your energy just to survive.

◆ Try to eat a balanced diet. This seems paradoxical when you are not feeling very hungry, but your body is using up vast quantities of energy and needs nutritional resources. Lean on others here. Tell them you hate to eat alone. Invite them over for a light meal, provided you don't have to go to any trouble. Check take-out restaurants for easy ideas. If a meal is too much trouble, invite someone over for tea or a glass of wine. You may later eat together anyhow.

◆ Seek out self-help groups, if you're ready again for group situations (Widow-to-Widow, Compassionate Friends, etc.). Members give support to one another by providing encouragement, pertinent information, and practical suggestions for managing grief. Their support can be invaluable at a time when you feel alone and different from other people. Churches usually offer study groups, which are often support groups in disguise. (Groups don't appeal to everyone, so don't worry if this remedy is not your bag.)

◆ Don't try to predict how long this very painful phase will take. It varies from person to person, situation to situation. Try to ride it out, knowing that it won't last forever. After losing something precious, the world looks dismal and bleak. Realizing—fully realizing—that the loss has taken place is what causes the agony. There is no shortcut for dealing with the pain of loss, but recognizing that it won't last forever will give you enough faith in yourself to keep on going.

◆ Don't conclude that you are going crazy; it just seems like you are, at times. This feeling *will* pass.

4

The Third Phase:
Conservation and the Need to Withdraw

Well, right about last November, I hit a real low period.
Up until then, I was doing real well, no tears or anything . . . then one week it was sudden-like. I just sunk.
I don't know why. I kept thinking to myself, "You should
be gettin' better by now, not worse." But I did feel worse,
like I needed to lie down and rest more often . . . just
real tired. So I did, anytime I felt bad. I thought I had
some kind of sickness . . . but eventually, it must have
passed. But it took a long time.

Widower, age 72

Just when we think we have
grieved all we possibly can and have cried enough tears for a
lifetime of sorrows, we move into a period that is frighten-
ingly like depression. This is the phase of withdrawal; we
need time to conserve what little energy we have left, before
we become completely exhausted. The previous phase of
awareness of loss, marked by volatile emotions, takes a toll
on our energy supplies and leaves us worn out both physically and emotionally. Our bodies desperately need rest and
restoration.

Let's look at how withdrawal works. Nancy's mother
suffered a stroke and died shortly after. Because she had
always been healthy throughout her sixty-nine years, no one

expected anything like this to happen. She had suffered no symptoms before the stroke; it was sudden and devastating. Paralysis afflicted her right side, so her speech was badly impaired, but at least she was conscious. No one at the hospital, including her doctors, expected her to die. They said things like "She's healthy and robust. She'll pull through." Or, "She's always had a marvelous positive attitude. This will help her now."

It didn't. Seventy hours after the stroke, Nancy's mother took her last breath. There were no heroics—she had signed a living will several years before. Nancy knew her mother well enough to know that she would never have tolerated the half-life she would have had to endure with the paralysis of the stroke. Nancy had little guilt, but enormous shock. "How can I live in a world without her?" she asked, weeping. "I have leaned on her forever. She was my security in so many ways—certainly my emotional security."

Nancy grieved her loss deeply, for months. She joined a bereavement support group and shared over and over the sadness and pain she felt. Her tears were endless. Nancy worried that she would never get over her mother's death, and her friends began to share that worry.

Around nine months after the death, long after Nancy felt she should be getting over her grief, she became increasingly lethargic. There wasn't enough energy to do much of anything, except go to work and do small maintenance chores at home. She wanted to sleep all the time. A sense of despair, of hopelessness about her own future, pervaded her thinking. Nancy felt that a deep depression was descending on her and she had no power to escape it.

She called me one day and said, "This is really getting me down. Just when I thought I should be getting better, I'm feeling worse. I want to sleep all the time. I feel exhausted. It really scares me. It's not normal. Usually I have more strength."

What was happening to Nancy was natural and normal. Rather than the clinical depression that Nancy feared, her body was showing a need to slow down and conserve energy. She had exhausted herself in the awareness-of-loss phase of her bereavement. The adrenaline flood had caused her bodily systems to race, over a prolonged period. She was left completely depleted. What looked like depression was actually a hibernation time that was necessary for rest and renewal. If Nancy had not responded to her body's message and instead had pushed herself harder, she might have done real damage to herself physically.

CHARACTERISTICS OF THE CONSERVATION AND NEED-TO-WITHDRAW PHASE

◆ Withdrawal and the need to rest
◆ Despair rather than depression
◆ Diminished social support
◆ Helplessness/loss of control

Withdrawal and the Need to Rest

This phase of grief may be your worst. Your emotional state will seem more like depression than anything you have experienced before in your bereavement. You will feel listless, fatigued, and full of despair. During this period, you will be content to stay alone more. You will feel like pulling back from your friends, even though, only a short time before, you relied on them to be with you a great deal of the time. You will have a tendency to push yourself beyond your physical limits, simply to reassure yourself and others that you are not depressed.

Despair Rather Than Depression

Time and time again, we wish for our beloved person to be back with us. We yearn, bargain, and search for any sign that they might be near, but all of this effort fails. Intellectually, we know that the lost person is dead; emotionally, we have not been convinced. The admission is too painful. We still long for and need that person in our lives. With repeated failure to get what we want, life begins to be dismal and overwhelmingly frustrating. Exhaustion takes over our mind and body, and a sense of utter despair creeps over us. We realize, as the deadening weight in our hearts grows heavier, that we are helpless to change this hopeless and tragic event.

This is a time of turning inward, of facing the loss, and of reviewing the earlier years spent together. The quiet truth is that the life we lived until the loss will never be regained; the beloved person in that life is gone forever. The hopelessness in that realization is the true meaning of despair.

Diminished Social Support

Most people give lovingly and freely of themselves when there has been a death. Unfortunately, their giving doesn't last long enough. There has been a gross underestimate of how long recovery from grief takes. Somehow the word got out that grief should be over in six months and the bereaved person should then be "back to normal." How wrong that estimate is.

A significant loss takes years to resolve. *We need support for our grief for as long as it takes.* The time each person needs will vary, depending on the closeness of the relationship and the other variables we discussed in Chapter 1. What usually happens is that the time, energy, and nurturance that friends provide shortly after the death taper off quickly. Friends and family members expect that grief should be over long before it really is. Intolerance for our situation creeps in, and we consciously try to get over it sooner. Grief can't be hurried. Try as we might to overcome it faster, the process will take exactly the time it requires.

Helplessness/Loss of Control

We feel out of control when there is nothing more to be done and when nothing that is done matters anyhow. Because control was essential to me, my grief was even more intolerable. The sheer frustration of my helplessness after my son's death left me despairing; I was sure that nothing would ever matter again. I could not change the fact of loss; Jim was gone and nothing I ever did would bring him back. I felt depleted and empty, like one of those inflated stand-up punching-bag clowns, when the air gradually escapes and it sinks slowly to the floor in a heap.

One of my first important lessons of bereavement was that I can't control the outcome of events in my life. I learned that the more I let go of the notion of control, the greater freedom I'll have to live and to love all those who are still around me. This lesson takes a long time to come into clear focus. I'm still working on it.

PHYSICAL SYMPTOMS OF THE CONSERVATION AND NEED-TO-WITHDRAW PHASE

◆ Weakness
◆ Fatigue
◆ Need for more sleep
◆ Weakened immune system

Weakness

There are times during this phase of bereavement when we become so weak that we actually feel like we have the flu. Because of our lack of experience with energy depletion, this weakness frightens and perplexes us. Before the loss, it happened only when we were sick.

I remember sitting on one end of the couch for hours, just staring into space. The thought of doing anything was almost impossible at these times. As months passed, I would be able to get something done but never with any enthusiasm or energy. Other people have told me of getting out the vacuum cleaner and then just sitting there looking at it, not able to even lift the handle. When we have led active lives, this weakness adds to our already intense feelings of inadequacy.

Fatigue

Most of the participants in the Tampa Study described this phase as one of debilitating fatigue. Not enough energy is available to get through the simplest of schedules. There seems to be an accompanying irritability that often borders on anger. Mary Ellen's husband died in an automobile accident on his way home from work one rainy night. She had heard the ambulances going by her house, but didn't know anything about the accident until she was called by hospital personnel, too late to see her husband alive. She said:

> It's been a year and a half and I still can't get the sounds of that night out of my head. They go round and round. I have to go to work every day and act as if I am fine, and do my job without making mistakes, but sometimes I could just scream. What do they expect of me, anyhow? When I get home at night, I'm finished. I can't do anything. I often just get a bowl of cereal and then go to bed. The days wear me out. . . . I don't know. . . . I wonder if I'll ever have any strength again.

Need for More Sleep

Up to this point, we have had trouble sleeping. Our alarm reaction was active enough to keep the adrenaline flowing;

our systems stayed alert to whatever danger might be in store. In the conservation and need-to-withdraw phase, there is a marked difference. We can't seem to get enough sleep—a frightening turnabout, if we aren't aware of what is taking place in our bodies. We are afraid that we are trying to use sleep as an escape or are giving in to depression. The truth is quite the opposite. The message is clear that our bodies need more rest immediately and we need to give in to this restorative process.

The accidental death of a promising young attorney left his wife shocked and inconsolable. She experienced the shock phase of bereavement for nearly a year, and the awareness-of-loss phase was equally prolonged. When she entered the conservation and need-to-withdraw phase, she was near complete exhaustion. She began sleeping for long periods of time, often napping in the afternoon and then going to bed at 6:00 or 7:00 in the evening. This routine frightened her because she had never needed much sleep before. She had always stayed up until her children were in bed. Now, she felt that she was not taking proper care of them. This guilt added tremendously to her grief, but she felt helpless to control her near-addiction to sleep. Worried over her health, she underwent a complete physical exam by her internist and was given a clean bill of health. After she learned that sleep was an adaptive response that was facilitating her recovery, she was able to not feel guilty or afraid when long hours of sleep were necessary.

We should all allow proper time for rest and should not put limitations on ourselves. A physical checkup is recommended, to make sure that no health complications are developing.

Weakened Immune System

Grief is a major cause of stress, which, in turn, produces changes in blood pressure, heart rate, and the chemical makeup of the blood. There is an indication that prolonged grief actually suppresses our immune system, leaving us exposed to a variety of illnesses, infections, and maladies. Under the impact of prolonged stress, our corticosteroid production is increased. This excess secretion then acts to suppress our bodies' immune mechanisms, causing us to be at considerable risk of illness or even death.

The sequence works this way. When a death occurs to someone close to us, we become wary and afraid. We feel that there is no safe place for us anywhere, and that our lives are out of control. We set up defensive forces within ourselves and become extra-alert to everything around us. This mobilization is followed by a stage of resistance: we try to adjust to the situation at hand. During this stage, our bodies are trying to repair themselves and gain some balance again. The continued stress of grief, however, doesn't supply an opportunity for restoration. If we are allowed to continue to the stage of exhaustion, there is the possibility that the resources we normally use for adaptation will have been used up and disease or death will be the outcome.

These are good reasons for taking care of ourselves during a major loss. The paradox we face is that, no matter what warnings we receive, we don't really care about ourselves. Our thoughts and ruminations are on the beloved person and the ended life we have lost.

PSYCHOLOGICAL ASPECTS OF THE CONSERVATION AND NEED-TO-WITHDRAW PHASE

◆ Hibernation
◆ Obsessional review
◆ Grief work
◆ Turning point

Hibernation

In this phase, we feel locked into a holding pattern, with no progress being made. We are stagnating. The world is moving on without us, and we are left behind with our pain, trying to make some sense out of our tragic loss. Our entire world is in chaos.

Despair hits us the deepest during this emotional hibernation. In our fear, we often try to accelerate the progress of our bereavement recovery, but this effort yields only more frustration. The truth remains: grief can't be hurried.

Our friends often become afraid for us and urge us to get busier. They advise, "This will get your mind off things. We'll spend the day shopping and have a wonderful time." (If you don't feel up to that kind of day, say no.) Overextending energies at this time can have dangerous side effects. We still need considerable rest.

Our loss has undermined our confidence in the world, leaving us insecure and afraid. A part of ourself is gone and everything that is left is meaningless and irrelevant. Life no longer seems to make any sense. Yet, even as we are caught in this holding pattern, we are actually moving forward toward resolution. The ruminations that we experience almost constantly are an important part of our grief work. We identified grief work earlier as gradually letting go of our beloved person and acknowledging the fact that the old conditions are no longer available to us. Our lives will never be the same again.

Obsessional Review

Our minds work wonders for us. They filter out what they don't want to deal with. The loss of a beloved person can't be realized suddenly. It takes time to understand emotionally that the person is gone forever. No matter how much we wish or yearn, no matter how many dreams return a beloved presence, reality coldly and harshly confirms the fact that our beloved person is dead. This testing of reality finally permits us to face the finality of our loss.

Resolution slowly begins to take place in our thoughts. By going over and over the life that we shared with our beloved person, we begin to find a starting place for our own individual life. Only when we realize fully that the loss has occurred and is permanent are we at a place where we can begin again. New assumptions must replace old ones. We must start here, in our emptiness, to somehow build a meaningful, purposeful world once again.

Grief Work

Obsessive ruminations are a necessary part of working through our grief. There was no shortcut to avoid the pain of grief; neither is there a shortcut to avoid the ruminations. Emotional venting was necessary during the awareness-of-loss phase of our grief; grief work is central to the conservation phase. In doing the work of grief—the ruminating and unfocused concentrating—there finally comes an understanding that the old conditions are gone. Life will never be the same as it was before.

Success in grief work depends on accepting the loss and the changes that will have to take place in our lives. We need to absorb the idea that we will need to find substitutes and replacements but do not have to give up precious memories.

Grief work gives us a death-and-resurrection experience. As we die to our old life, a new one is being forged in its place.

Turning Point

Slowly, we begin to reach a welcome turning point. Just when we think that we cannot bear another day in limbo, something happens: a new event emerges, or we simply wake up one morning and realize that we are feeling a little more hopeful. The long-awaited turning point of grief has come. We will begin gradually to move toward the resolution that we had doubted would ever come.

The turning point comes toward the end of the conservation and need-to-withdraw phase. If we make a decision to move forward with our lives, we will feel the first, tenuous glimmer of hope. If we, instead, decide that we don't have the energy to adjust to a new life, then we will probably keep things pretty much as they are for us. We will act as though the beloved person is away on a trip and will return eventually.

ENDING THE CONSERVATION AND NEED-TO-WITHDRAW PHASE

Our main tasks during this stage are to accept the reality of the loss and to resolve the conflicts of grief. The greatest conflict involves whether we can make the decision to move on with our lives or must instead remain in chronic bereavement.

When you are working through this phase, these actions are important:

◆ Give yourself permission to withdraw from others. You need quiet and restorative time to do the important work of coming to terms with your loss. This grief work can't be done when you are surrounded with people or distracted by other interests. Grief requires your attention.

◆ Recognize your need to conserve energy. Healing begins with the restoration of your body. When you understand the shock you have experienced and the resulting stress caused by loss, you can see that grief is similar to an amputation. You would never think of pushing yourself immediately after losing a limb. You would, instead, allow time for healing to take place.

◆ Create opportunities to sleep more. When you feel sleepy, your body is giving you a clear message that you need to rest more. Cat naps or more hammock time are part of recovery.

◆ Allow ruminations to happen. Go over and over the events of the death, the years of life together, the pros and cons of the lost relationship, the countless memories (good and bad) that are stored in your mind. Eventually, you will finally be able to release the deceased.

◆ Take this as the time to look at photos—to really *look* at them and relive the meaning behind each one. If they are not in albums, now might be a good time to catalog them and organize albums until you run out of pictures. Recording your life puts it in perspective.

◆ Nurture yourself with things you like: good food and wine, flowers (a bouquet of daisies from the supermarket is fine), some special flavors of tea, deep baths full of lovely fragrance or long showers that pepper your body and relax you. Try a massage. This is the time of early healing and your body needs to be nourished in many ways.

◆ Ride out the low periods knowing that they are getting shorter all the time.

◆ Recognize that you are mourning not only the person you loved but the way of life you knew for years.

◆ Be alert to any dependency behavior you are indulging in because you are a bereaved person. Fiercely rid yourself of the behavior or the attitudes that are promoting it.

◆ Give in to feelings of fatigue. If they seem to be excessive, arrange for a checkup by your physician—not a bad idea even without the fatigue.

◆ Simplify your life. Find shortcuts for everything possible.

◆ Shift around some furniture in your house, as a first step toward realizing a need for change in your home environment. Other changes will follow more easily.

◆ Reassure yourself that you are not going crazy. You just feel at times as though you are.

5

The Fourth Phase: Healing—The Turning Point

About two years after the death, I started to keep a daily account of my feelings. I tried to write at the times I needed to "let go" of my emotions. I only found it necessary to keep this for about two months on a daily basis, and then very seldom. It was a way of releasing my feelings without hurting or upsetting someone else's feelings. It also showed me that I was beginning to "come back to life."

Widow, age 37

Mrs. Moore had been married to a prominent physician for thirty-five years. All her life, she had loved her role of doctor's wife. Her community work and social life had revolved around her husband's status and profession. Her schedule was patterned to fit his. Often, she waited until late in the evening, hoping to have dinner with him; she would finally get sleepy and go to bed. She always tolerated his delays with a good nature. He had a wonderful way with people, she said.

During a particularly busy January, Dr. Moore, as usual, left his home for the hospital at 5:30 A.M. After making rounds, he arrived at his office around 9:45 A.M. He hung up his coat and began to change into his white lab coat. Then a heart attack struck, quickly and lethally. Even with the resuscitation efforts of his medical associates, nothing could be done. The massiveness of the attack was too great to alter.

Dr. Moore's closest friend and associate, Dr. Phelps, offered to go in person to tell Mrs. Moore. She was getting ready to go to an auxiliary luncheon when Dr. Phelps drove up. Mrs. Moore knew by his expression that something awful had happened. But she was a strong woman and, after the initial shock, pulled herself together and even comforted Dr. Phelps. She got through the rituals somehow; friends marveled at how she managed it all. She wondered about it herself: was she doing it herself or watching herself go through all the motions?

Her bereavement, however, was a different story. The first year was manageable somehow. Mrs. Moore was a stoic person who did not allow others to see her grieve. The second year was more difficult; by the third year, she was lost. Her volunteer jobs were becoming grinding obstacle courses. Tasks she had once loved now irritated her. She felt uncomfortable when she was with couples. She had less and less to share with her friends, and it was painful to hear their stories of holidays and trips together. She could not imagine why she had been left here, to live on without her husband. Her entire world had collapsed.

Mrs. Moore, in desperation, decided to take a trip alone. The group she had traveled with during the past two years was getting monotonous. She often found herself bored when she was with them, and she began valuing her times alone more highly. One May day, she set out on a trip to the Southwest by car, telling only her daughter where she was heading.

After a week or so of touring Grand Canyon and other beautiful spots, she stopped at a ranch for about two weeks. There, she began to catch up with herself and survey her life. The two weeks offered her a turning point in her bereavement and in her life. From this faraway place, she gained a new perspective on what her life had become during the years of her marriage. Without her husband, there was no focus; she had no identity. She had been Dr. Moore's wife for so long that she had forgotten how to be Maggie Moore, a person in her own right. She knew now that, for the past three years, she had been an empty shell echoing the past. She now had to live her own life. She needed to find out who she was and what she wanted to do with the rest of her years. This was her breakthrough, her turning point in bereavement. Healing had begun.

CHARACTERISTICS OF THE HEALING PHASE
◆ Reaching a turning point
◆ Assuming control
◆ Relinquishing roles
◆ Forming a new identity
◆ Centering ourselves

Reaching a Turning Point

Bereavement has a turning point, but it is hard to determine where it is and when we've reached it. There are no clearly defined marks of change, no sudden leaps of the heart or quick accelerations in activity. Instead, we have a slowly dawning awareness that a little more energy is available. We seem willing to do a few more things. We aren't getting tired as quickly as we did only a few long months ago. People have said to me, "I realized that something was different; I didn't feel as tired or depressed as before," or, "I don't think I was aware of any one thing—there was just a slight change in my attitude. I felt a little lighter." Mrs. Tragar, whose husband died at fifty-seven of lung cancer, talked about her feelings when she reached the turning point:

> I can't pinpoint it. It was just kind of . . . nothing that's dramatic. It's been a gradual thing. It didn't happen overnight. I didn't just wake up one morning and say, Well,

I'm not going to do it anymore. I'm not going to think about it (death). It's not going to bother me. I think it's how you deal with it twenty-four hours a day. I don't think about him less. I think about him differently, but not less. I think about him mostly as alive—when our memories were happy.

Sometimes, an external event makes a difference in turning our grief around—a vacation gives us a new perspective, a new job moves us from one environment to another, or a return to school takes us into a completely different atmosphere. Anything that lifts us out of our rut and places us in a different routine, or around new people, can make a difference in how we perceive the world.

A specific event might push us to the turning point by making us angry enough to act on our current feelings. When Mrs. Blake's husband died of cancer, she refused to leave her house. Friends and neighbors went grocery shopping for her and took care of the various things she needed done. When I called on her only a few weeks after her husband's death, her shades were drawn and she was in her robe. She told me, "I have given up dressing; don't want to see anyone. I just want to stay here." And she was very firm about these choices.

Nearly a year later, however, Mrs. Blake got caught up in some social security red tape concerning a hospital bill. The social security office said she hadn't paid it and she knew she had. One day, after a particularly frustrating phone conversation with a social security representative, she got so angry that she dressed herself, got in her car, and drove all the way across town to the social security office. In person, she settled her case once and for all. Satisfied, she got in her car and drove home again. She had become so angry with the representative that she had forgotten about herself. She didn't even realize what she had done until she was on her way home. She had managed to turn her anger away from herself momentarily, in order to focus it outward. When she forgot herself, her anger and determination motivated her to take action. This broke the stranglehold of grief. After that, she began going out more often and became less fearful.

Assuming Control

Taking control of our lives again after a major bereavement can be a frightening task, especially if it means making drastic changes. Adapting to changes is hard enough under any circumstances, but when we are just beginning to heal and haven't regained our confidence, changes look even more imposing than at other times. We have a real fear that any decision we reach might make our situation worse, so we lapse into no action at all and we create an even greater problem of stagnation. Somehow it feels safer to take no action and maintain a familiar status quo.

For many of us, trying to assume control of our lives when we're not ready to do it dooms the attempt. Failure may result in a sense of continued helplessness. One young mother, whose child had died of leukemia, decided to take her old job back and return to school at the same time. She was determined that she could end her grief. She didn't want to hurt anymore. This attempt, unfortunately, led her to take on too much. She became constantly irritated with her children, her husband, and her co-workers. Her continued stress plummeted her back into the despair of the conservation and need-to-withdraw phase again. Not until she received professional help could she see what she was doing to herself.

Gaining a sense of control comes slowly, often in bits and pieces. We need to remind ourselves that the healing process is one of slow repair. It doesn't happen overnight.

Relinquishing Roles

Within the family system, prescribed roles are set for each member. Mother, father, oldest child, youngest child, and every niche in between is taken by one person and one person only. With each of these roles comes a share in the tasks and responsibilities that keep the family going and provide stability for the system. Each person is connected to every other member in a different way. The balance is delicate; it depends on the system's remaining intact and making no changes. When one of the family leaves or the balance changes in any way, the family system goes through a period of readjustment. Certain roles must be shifted to another member or relinquished altogether. Giving up our roles is one of the hardest tasks of bereavement.

When my children were all young, I had a definite pattern as I pushed the shopping cart through the supermarket. Usually, for our size family (four children and a great dane), I would need two shopping carts. My stop in the cereal section, for example, took a fairly long time because I always bought several brands for Jim as well as the brands everyone else liked. Cold cereal was snack food in our household. Jim liked to eat it when he came home from school or before he went to bed.

After Jim was killed, shopping became a heartbreaking experience. I had to avoid the cereal section or I would sob profusely; many times, I left the store before I finished my shopping. Birthday cards affected me the same way. I realized I would never again buy a card that said "Happy Birthday, Son." With Jim's death, my identity had changed—a part of me had died. I was no longer the mother of a seventeen-year-old son. As a matter of fact, I was no longer the caregiver for a large family. Sue and Sally were both beginning separate lives, and Jim would never be back. It was the worst period of my life. To survive, I had to rethink my entire world view. I was becoming a different person, although I didn't know it at the time. Slowly, I was to learn that changes in my whole world needed to be made.

Forming a New Identity

When we suffer a major loss, we are faced with a crisis transition much like the one we experienced in adolescence. Getting our sea legs as teenagers, we fluctuated between being haughtily independent and being childishly in need of our parents. Maturity came when we accepted the responsibility of a new and different life, depending more on ourselves and our own decisions than on our parents. All transitions thereafter were similar. With bereavement, we regress; our confidence is eroded and we become frightened of a world in which we have lost control. It seems easier to hide and do nothing rather than risk making a poor judgment or a mistake. On the other hand, doing nothing means stagnation. There is no possibility for growth.

Gerald Corey writes about this in his book, *Theory and Practice of Counseling and Psychotherapy:*

> The trouble with so many of us is that we have sought directions, answers, values, and beliefs in the important people in our worlds rather than trusting ourselves to search within and find our own answers to the conflicts in our lives; we sell out by becoming what others expect of us. Our being becomes rooted in their being and we become strangers to ourselves.

Our biggest task in bereavement is to carve out a new life based on what we need for ourselves. Many bereaved people are strangers to themselves and are groping blindly, moving from one distraction to another. Bereavement offers us the opportunity to find ourselves once again.

Centering Ourselves

We can't begin the task of restructuring ourselves without first going through the process of centering ourselves. Without the centering process, we have no idea of how we really feel, what we need for ourselves, or what we want to do. Centering ourselves does not mean being egotistical or self-centered in the derogatory sense. Instead, it means that we find our own center of stability. We must trust that we can make decisions for ourselves based on *our* needs and values, not someone else's. To do this, we need to learn about and get to know ourselves as fully as we can.

Grief was placed on us. We didn't ask for it, but it nevertheless was handed to us. What we do with our grief is a different matter. We have the choice of living in the past, still married to our old identities, or of moving on to find what life has to offer. It is imperative that, before we move too fast, we begin to search for our own core, our unique center. We will be blocked from seeing the importance of our lives if we fail to discover that we are the center of our lives. Being centered in our own life gives us the confidence to actively work out our own crises and problems. Centering helps us to feel in place in our lives—not leaning on others for support, but having the strength to stand on our own two legs.

In their wonderful book, *Shifting Gears,* Nena and George O'Neill write about the centering process:

> Being centered is like riding a bike. The feeling of knowing your center of balance and feeling sure of yourself is the same. Now riding a bike doesn't take much; almost anyone can do it. But you must get it rolling and risk falling before you can experience balancing. No one can do it for you; you must find that inner sense of balance for yourself. Having once learned it, you never forget it and your mastery of the bike enables you to move that bike in the direction you want to go. Having once learned to center, you find that inner sense of confidence and belief in yourself that enables you to be more flexible, yet more certain that you can manage your decisions, actions, crises and growth in a positive way.

PHYSICAL SYMPTOMS OF THE HEALING PHASE

◆ Physical healing
◆ Increased energy
◆ Sleep restoration
◆ Stronger immune system

Physical Healing

Biologically, our bodies are healing themselves during this phase. Gradually, the prolonged stress that we have been under during the first three phases is beginning to ease. Our bodies have gained some rest and we are beginning to experience a more positive attitude. These improvements, in turn, create new energy sources for further healing. We sense a time of rebirth, a shedding of some of the physical and emotional weight of grief.

Increased Energy

We will naturally develop more energy as we develop better health. As this happens, it is important to maintain a moderate exercise program as well as a nutritious diet. We need to begin to strengthen our bodies and add some necessary diversion to our lives. I found that I sat a lot when I was in deepest grief. Being immobile tended to make me feel lethargic way past the time when I should have been gaining more energy.

Sleep Restoration

Stress prevents restful sleep. During the particularly painful phases of bereavement, we are producing hormones that serve to prepare us for action. As stress lessens, our sleep patterns return to normal. If our sleep patterns have been broken for a prolonged period of time, we may need to work on restoring them. By learning techniques such as yoga, progressive relaxation, and self-hypnosis, we can help ourselves to become relaxed and sleepy. Being able to master these methods will restore a sense of control over ourselves. We will feel safer.

Stronger Immune System

Our renewed feelings of safety and security, growing slowly now, act to strengthen our bodies during this phase. We find that we are having fewer health problems than in the beginning of our bereavement. As our stress level diminishes, our immune system is strengthened and we become less susceptible to colds and flu. Surviving a major bereavement is in many ways like reversing the aging process. Instead of a gradual deterioration of health resources, as in the aging process, we find that these resources gradually increase with time. The saying "Time heals all wounds" can be seen in this light as applying to our bodies as well as our emotions.

PSYCHOLOGICAL ASPECTS OF THE HEALING PHASE

- ◆ Forgiving
- ◆ Forgetting
- ◆ Searching for meaning
- ◆ Closing the circle
- ◆ Renewing hope

Forgiving

"I'll never forgive myself for not insisting that John see a doctor." "Why didn't I take those first warning symptoms seriously, when Alice came home from school early last May?" "How did I ever allow Bobby to take the car out on such a rainy night and only a week after he got his license?"

In all these cases, bereaved individuals found it hard to forgive themselves. Some of us may have experienced similar regrets, and we know how painful and disturbing these terrible thoughts are. They can plague us for months, or even years, before we are finally willing to forgive ourselves for our deeds of omission or commission. Usually, during the healing phase of grief, we are finally able to let go of this source of pain.

Forgiveness works in two ways. First, it allows us to work through emotions such as guilt, anger, and shame, which were there when we blamed ourselves, in some way, for the death. We also must forgive ourselves for surviving—for not being the one to die.

Second, we need to forgive the one who died—for leaving us and causing such suffering and agony. Forgiving our loved one is harder than forgiving ourselves, because it is often done at the unconscious level. Loneliness and frustration take a toll on our reserve energy and we are often depleted or exhausted when these feelings of forgiveness take over.

Forgiveness comes slowly, bit by bit. Once realized, it can be a blessed emancipation.

Forgetting

Forgetting implies "letting go." But how can we ever let go of our beloved person? This has got to be one of the hardest tasks of bereavement. When we have been strongly attached to someone, having to let go of that person becomes impossibly painful. It rocks the very foundation of our worst fear—a fear of abandonment. We are thrown back into our childhood trauma all over again. This is why grief feels so like fear. That terrible memory of abandonment haunts us all. But it is in the act of saying good-bye to the past, to the unrequited yearning and longing to be with our dear one, that grief work can finally be resolved.

The Foresters had been married for forty-four years when Mr. Forester died of colon cancer. After grieving intensely for the first year, Mrs. Forester was now, fourteen months after the death, trying to deal with her grief without crying all the time. Lately, she had discovered that the best way for her to manage was to remove her husband's things from view. This was in no way a denial of his death, but she found she cried less if she was not constantly reminded of it. Mrs. Forester told me that a friend of hers had asked why she did not have her husband's picture displayed. She answered, "Because I'm trying to forget him." She went on to tell me:

> I don't know whether that's being inhuman or not, but I'm really trying to forget him. I don't dwell on bad things. I don't have any pictures around. I don't have any of his things around at all. I really don't. And it's not that I want to go with somebody else, you know what I mean. It's just that it's my way of coping and surviving.

Mrs. Forester's resolution to stop crying became a shift point in her bereavement process. In saying that she was trying to forget her husband, she meant that she was trying to let go of her wish to have him back, to stop herself from yearning for him the way she had during her first year of grief. She was not trying to forget the wonderful forty-four years of marriage; they were very precious to her. But she did want to let go of the suffering of grief, the unrequited longing that had kept her locked into the past. When she put away his things, Mrs. Forester was, in essence, looking toward a new life in the future.

Forgetting doesn't mean that we will not experience poignant memories from time to time, or that anniversary reactions will be erased. If we were to remove all memories (as if we ever could), we would be wiping out the meaning of all the beautiful times we shared with our beloved person as well as the meaning of that person's life. Forgetting is actually appropriate remembering.

Letting go refers to the act of turning to new encounters and trusting in the future. When we can do this, we establish expectations that move us toward the rebuilding of a life with new rewards and reinforcements.

Searching for Meaning

Early in my grief, if anyone had said that I could ever find meaning in Jim's death—or that of any other family member I lost—I would have been incredulous. Few of us who have suffered a significant loss have been able to find comfort in this experience initially. Before we can possibly extract some meaning from the death, we need to be able to process what the person meant to us and to others. In the first phases of grief, we don't have the perspective to do this. We fill our head with cul-de-sacs by asking "Why?" over and over, and we have no ready answers.

Yet, our search for meaning in the death goes on relentlessly until we can find some peace in a justifiable conclusion. Often, this peace comes when we do something to memorialize our beloved person's life. Margaret volunteered in the cancer ward where her husband died. She was able to comfort other families who were going through a similar situation. Carrie, whose beautiful seventeen-year-old daughter was killed in a car accident, courageously started a chapter of Compassionate Friends and told her story many times, in order to bring solace to others. The list goes on and on. Each time we offer ourselves in a caring manner, we create some meaning for our lives while at the same time memorializing our beloved person.

The outstanding characteristic of bereaved people is that they generally become more compassionate toward others who are suffering a loss of any kind. Mr. Powell never went to funerals before his wife died. He didn't believe in them—they were "morbid." When Mrs. Powell died, he saw them a different way. He was grateful for each and every person who came to see him or dropped a note. He felt supported, and was enormously comforted to see how his wife was loved. Now, he tells me, he never misses an opportunity to help a bereaved person. He learned how important it is to feel the kindness and consideration of others when we feel so broken.

We may find the greatest peace by exploring what our beloved person's life has meant. Sometimes, it is helpful to put together a photo album of all our pictures of the person, or a scrap book of mementos. By doing this, we are able to see the chronology of events and get a more complete view of the person's life. Friends may have photos or personal stories that can be included in either book.

No matter what other things we do, we still have the need to talk about our loved one, to tell the stories over and over, and to relate funny little incidents that we witnessed. This is still the best antidote to grief. Friends who continue to listen to us and share our feelings are among the most priceless gifts we can be given.

For some bereaved persons, the greatest gift during grief will come through a spiritual connection. Reestablishing our faith in God or our higher power and trusting in the love He offers can give us a sense of peace that is difficult to find anywhere else.

Closing the Circle

Closing the circle is synonymous to closing the wound; it signifies the true meaning of healing. Scar tissue will remain, probably permanently, but the open wound is closing. Many primitive societies have rituals and ceremonies that symbolize the new unit. Families close the circle by joining hands, sharing a ritual meal, or burning sacrificial foliage that creates dense smoke to represent the departing spirit. In each case, the purpose is to separate the living from the dead. The survivors are then released to continue their lives with a new commitment.

Unfortunately, our society provides few rituals that give the bereaved this bridge to the future. The funeral is over too soon to offer a sense of finality. It generally marks only the beginning of grief. Closing the circle then has to be done in less symbolic ways, such as beginning to associate with newfound friends who were not a part of life before the death.

Alma and her husband, Jim, lived in a small midwestern town for most of their thirty-two years of married life. Jim had joined a firm early in his career and had done well for his family. All four children had finished college, and his second son, George, had joined him in the business. Alma had always been active in clubs and organizations in the community. She and Jim were constantly busy with social activities. They were a popular couple among their friends. The news of Jim's illness came as a terrible blow to everyone. He had always been so healthy, so robust. The fact that he could have a malignant melanoma was unthinkable; he still looked well and felt OK. The disease moved swiftly. Inside four months, Jim was dead.

The town was stunned but reacted with tremendous support and love. Alma was included in the same group and continued to be a part of the activities she was involved in before the death. Everyone admired the way she dealt with her grief—stoically, bravely, comforting others who were bereaved. Her children rallied around her. That first year, she had all the support she could use.

It wasn't until the third year that she began to notice how little she had in common with her couple friends. They talked about vacations, business trips, or things that they were doing together. She tried to build in single activities for herself, such as courses at the local community college or volunteering for political campaigns. At a political rally, she met an attorney from the state capital. As they discussed election strategies, they uncovered other activities that they could share. He had been divorced two years before, after a long marriage, and was only interested in friendship, which exactly suited Alma's thoughts.

They began to see each other on weekends and enjoyed their time together immensely. Because Alma was busier, she wasn't able to accept as many social engagements with her friends as before. She saw the wives at lunches but found that the couple activities were not so interesting now. Alma did not consciously realize that she was closing the circle. She was finding a new group of friends with whom she could share her current life. She didn't give up her old friends, but her new life depended on her living in the present, not the past.

Our need to find new ways of sharing life emerges slowly. For Alma, it surfaced in the third year after the death. For others, it might take five or ten years. Trying out new lifestyles can be scary and disappointing at times. We seek guarantees that will take the risk out of our efforts (and put us in better control over the outcome). But life doesn't offer us these safeguards and, if we are to progress, we have to take a deep breath and step out alone into our new life.

Renewing Hope

The very fact that we are beginning to have thoughts of a future, even if the thoughts are tenuous and uncertain, leads us to a fledgling feeling of hope. This marks the beginning of our being able to look back past the tragic events of the death to see the happy memories that we had with our beloved person. A more realistic view replaces the idealistic one that helped us through the earlier phases of bereavement. Idealization works very well for us when we need a balance for our ambivalent feelings. But idealization blocks a more complete picture of a person. Until we are able to let go of those "perfect" memories, we cannot admit the frailties as well as the strengths of the lost person. When we can finally think in these terms, we are ready to move on to the final phase of grief, that of renewal.

ENDING THE HEALING PHASE

These are the actions and realities to be conscious of during the healing phase:

◆ Be aware of small lifts in energy, even the slightest signs. Recognizing them will give you hope that there might be an end to your grief on the horizon.

◆ Be patient with yourself; grief takes time. It is understandable that you will want to rush the process, but it moves at its own pace.

◆ Make some decisions for yourself. Try to avoid being perfect. You will make mistakes, but generally you will manage more things right when you trust your own intuitions.

◆ Recognize the need to relinquish roles. Determine which ones you want to keep or which ones can be given up. As you streamline your own position in life, simplify the decisions you are called on to make. For example, if you have had to relinquish the role of wife, you might begin to accept the new identity of "me."

◆ Learn to be selfish. By that I mean you should think of your own needs alongside, or even ahead of, the needs of others. Only after you have learned to love yourself can you truly love others.

◆ Take care of your body. Exercise in a systematic manner. Walk, jog, do aerobics; any of these will do, but make sure you put yourself on a schedule. Their repetition will truly keep your body in condition.

◆ Eat properly. Stay away from fat, and focus on balanced meals. Once you get used to eating this way, your health and physical maintenance can be assured.

◆ Don't think you have to give up all your memories in order to resolve your grief. Memories are indications that a person lived, had an important place in your world, and shared your life. Keep alive the memories that help you to grow. They will strengthen you without interfering with the new life you must assume for yourself.

◆ Search out new acquaintances who interest you, and find ways to interact. Out of this larger group will surely come one or two friends whom you will enjoy.

◆ Take up a new hobby. Find an activity or skill that you have always wanted to try, and take a course at a nearby community college. I recently took a course in fencing. I will never be a competitor and may never pick up a foil again, but I learned the basic positions and movements and had fun doing it.

◆ Don't push yourself. Allow life to unfold in its own way. Take things gradually. Keep life simple.

◆ Allow yourself "time off" from your grief. Spend time with friends, laugh, enjoy the moment if it feels right. You don't need to feel disloyal when you have a good time. Respites will give you energy to complete your grief work.

◆ Search for meaning in the death. Only by fully resolving this issue can you let go of your loved one.

◆ Take time to center. Use meditation, stillness, prayer, psychotherapy, or any other method that helps you to go inward. To move toward a new identity, you'll need to find out what that identity is about. Centering won't give quick and easy answers, but it will start you on a valid search for your own truth.

6

The Fifth Phase: Renewal

> During this time of recovery, I learned many things
> about myself . . . mainly that I could cope. I found my-
> self able to do things and handle affairs which I never
> dreamed possible, and do them in a businesslike man-
> ner. I also became aware of the outside world around me
> instead of being in a sheltered world of homemaker.
> George would have been really surprised if he could see
> me now—maybe a little proud too. No, maybe a lot.
>
> *Widow, age 52*

We never believed that we
would reach this place. When the death occurred, life seemed
over for us. There was nothing out there: no future, no hope,
no vitality. All our strength was caught up in surviving, and
even that didn't matter too much at times. Blackness had
descended on us for what appeared to be forever.

Changes were taking place, however, even without our
knowing it. Slowly, we were coming to grips with a world
from which our beloved person was gone. Our many social
losses were dealt with one-by-one. We began to feel a little
stronger, and our self-esteem was growing. Whether we
wanted to or not, we were finding substitutes for our
beloved person—a new hobby, a volunteer job, college, or a
new friend who shared some of our interests. We filled our
time somehow. Soon, almost without knowing it, we became
ready to move to the final phase of bereavement: renewal.

Are we the same people as before the death? Far from it. The agony and emptiness of loss create scars that remain forever, but the burning pain, the unrequited yearning, and the endless "Why?" have subsided. We will still experience anniversary reactions and great loneliness from time to time. But, as we have moved away from the death, we have unconsciously opted for life. We know now that we must go forward to whatever lies ahead.

Grief is like a death-and-resurrection experience. As part of our old self dies with our old life, there is almost simultaneous preparation for a rebirth into a new one. When that new life comes, so does a new strength that fills it to capacity.

CHARACTERISTICS OF THE RENEWAL PHASE

◆ Renewing self-awareness
◆ Accepting responsibility for ourselves
◆ Learning to live without

Renewing Self-Awareness

In his book, *Transitions,* William Bridges says of new beginnings that we come to beginning only at the end. He writes, "It is when the endings and the time of fallow neutrality are finished that we can launch ourselves out anew, changed and renewed by the destruction of the old life-phase and the journey through the nowhere." Bridges makes an interesting observation regarding our mechanistic culture: we are used to starting things with a key or a switch. If they don't start properly and immediately, there must be something wrong.

After a significant loss, a period of transition must occur, to move us from one internal place to another. We need time to process all aspects of the deprivation we have suffered, before we are able to accept that there can be any new acquisitions. The real strength of grief comes from a new, if slowly arriving, self-awareness. We change without realizing it. Faced with few other options, we square our chin and reluctantly learn to deal with the situation on hand. We can see new alternatives opening up and we hold the freedom to choose. When we accept the freedom to select a way that is entirely our own, amazing things can happen. Susie lost her husband in a car accident after only eight years of marriage. She and George married right out of high school, so Susie moved from her Dad's taking care of her to her husband's doing the same. They quickly had two little boys. Before George was killed, Susie had no thought of going to work anytime soon. Afterward, she was forced to find some supplemental income. She told me:

> I hated it, having to go out and find work. I never felt so bad about myself before . . . so lacking in self-confidence. But I made myself; well, I had to because there just wasn't enough to go around. Getting out was a turning point for me, though. I got the first job I applied for, which was lucky. I liked the people there after I got over being nervous. I was very lucky but I had to go out after it; it didn't come to me. So, I guess I learned something.

For Susie, a new sense of competency emerged from an inner strength that she hadn't tapped before George's death. This loss was, by far, the worst thing that had ever happened to her. But, looking back on the past two years, she was proud that she had been able to show such stability and courage. Susie never dreamed she would be able to cope with anything so tragic and shattering as George's death or raising two active boys alone. She had done both.

Accepting Responsibility for Ourselves

Existentialists tell us that we are responsible for our own lives and destiny. They say we can neither escape loneliness nor be totally free. From their point of view, we are ultimately all alone anyhow and, unless we have learned a certain amount of independence before a significant loss, we'll be overwhelmed by fear and uncertainty when we find ourselves alone. Our worst fears of abandonment are suddenly renewed when we discover that we alone must give meaning to our lives.

Many of us feel confident that we can take care of ourselves. We are physically self-reliant, provide ourselves with clothing and shelter, keep our bodies fit, and handle our social needs. The area that causes us the most trouble when we must endure bereavement is our lack of emotional independence. (Men have a particularly hard job identifying emotional dependence.) We want someone else to meet our emotional needs rather than supplying them for ourselves. Our expectation seems perfectly natural. We identified first with our parents, later with our spouses, and then with our children. Our good feelings (or bad) depended on their feelings, how they reacted to us. We have given ourselves away to the important people around us. We continue to try to please them so that we can feel good and so that they won't leave us. If we make them unhappy, we risk isolation and abandonment. Learning to take care of personal emotional needs can become one of the most liberating experiences of a lifetime.

We must eventually learn to focus on positive aspects of our newfound freedom. In the beginning of grief, this need is hard to see. Like everything else in the process of bereavement, it takes a long time to come into focus. We usually have to confront our loneliness, meaninglessness, emptiness, guilt, and isolation to realize that we won't be overcome by them. After the confrontation, we become stronger and freer.

It isn't always easy for us to accept responsibility for our lives, especially if we have previously relied on others too heavily. However, the many lonely times we experience during grief slowly teach us: if we are to survive, we will need to take care of ourselves. There may be no one else to do it now.

Learning to Live Without

Losing a precious family member means learning to live without the resources we once took for granted: a husband or wife who filled our lives with meaning and purpose, a child who was an object of nurturance and love, a parent who was a lifelong role model. If we are to really begin a new life, we need to find substitutions and replacements to fill the emptiness caused by the death. Searching for substitutions can be disastrous if we try to do it before we are able to know that we can never find an exact replacement. For example, some people try to find a husband or wife who was just like the one who died. Parents have tried to replace a child by quickly having another and then trying to mold this child into the pattern of the one they lost. Naturally, if we have those attitudes toward substitutions, we will be sorely disappointed and miserable because an exact replica can never be found or created. To avoid this constant disappointment, we must work through our grief until we have reached a new level of functioning. Once our renewal is achieved, we can more wisely seek replacements, taking into consideration the change that has occurred within ourselves.

PHYSICAL SYMPTOMS OF THE RENEWAL PHASE

◆ Reenergizing ourselves
◆ Finding stability
◆ Taking care of our physical needs

Reenergizing Ourselves

In the renewal phase, we become aware that we have finally regained the energy lost in the beginning of bereavement. Having come through this interminable period of grief, it seems almost a miracle that we have survived. Grief has taken a toll. Yet, with a resurgence of vitality, however small, there comes a beginning of hope about the future. In the introduction to his *Collected Poems,* D. H. Lawrence wrote:

> Then, in that year, for me everything collapsed, save the mystery of death, and the haunting of death in life. I was twenty five, and from the death of my mother, the world began to dissolve around me, beautiful, iridescent, but passing away substanceless. Till I almost dissolved away myself and was very ill; when I was twenty six.
>
> Then slowly the world came back: or I myself returned: but to another world.

We are on our way back to the world again but it is a different world—not the world we would have chosen, had we been given the choice. We now have a little more energy with which to cope.

Finding Stability

Our erratic emotional outbursts of early grief have subsided and we feel more in control of ourselves. Biologically, our bodies have had time to heal and renew themselves. We feel a new strength, a strength that we perhaps didn't even know we possessed before the death. We have heard that a broken bone can heal to become even stronger than before. So it is with grief. The fact that we lived through the pain, the confusion, and the problems along the way notifies us that we are stronger than we thought we were. Special times such as anniversaries or holidays will still be painful and poignant, but the despair, helplessness, and hopelessness that we once felt have lifted. Our lives have taken on a calmer, more organized stability.

Taking Care of Our Physical Needs

We've been through the sleepless nights. We've felt the nausea that makes us lose any desire for food. We've known the exhaustion of middle grief, when we couldn't lift our arms to do another thing. These debilitating effects may still be with us from time to time, but, for the most part, we are feeling physically stronger. Our needs to have proper nutrition and good exercise continue. We are building preventive, protective mechanisms that will make us less vulnerable to trauma in the future.

There is an added advantage to taking better care of ourselves. Being in control of our lives once again brings renewed confidence. It is essential to our survival that we learn new health skills after a period of relative inactivity. Besides, joining a health club or aerobics class, or setting up a daily walk or jog, is a wonderful way to take continued care of ourselves.

PSYCHOLOGICAL ASPECTS OF THE RENEWAL PHASE

◆ Living for ourselves
◆ Enduring the anniversaries
◆ Focusing
◆ Keeping loneliness in perspective
◆ Reaching out
◆ Understanding the long process of grieving

Living for Ourselves

Learning to live for ourselves seems like a pretty boring occupation when we have spent a good part of our lives thinking of and doing for others. If we have nursed our beloved person through a long terminal illness, we face the "empty hands" syndrome. We took care of so many needs of our patient that the tasks became second nature to us. We feel that we have nothing to do now, no purpose in life. To devote time to ourselves seems like a waste of energy. We don't even know how to do it. If we have lived much of our lives through others—our spouses, our children, our parents—learning to live for ourselves means that we must begin to satisfy our own needs first. Or, as we saw in the previous chapter, we must learn to center ourselves, to turn our thoughts and energies inward toward taking care of our physical and spiritual selves. We can do this through a process of meditation, prayer, psychotherapy, reading, study, or anything that will head off life's constant distractors and move us toward a quieter place within ourselves.

Isabella Taves writes about this in her book, *Love Must Not be Wasted:*

> The early days of grief—although they may not seem so— are easier. Tears, anguish come spontaneously; people around you are understanding. There is also the cushion of shock, the courage that comes with unreality. The second part, the long road back, is more difficult. It consists of rehabilitating yourself, rebuilding your life with an eye to the future, destroying your old self so that you may live again. . . . but once again, if you accept the challenge of creating a new and more liberated life, your own growth will be your reward.

We are on the long road back now, and it does seem more difficult. Each time I lost a family member, I thought I would never reach the end of my grief. I finally saw that each loss would change me in a different way, and only then did I really see the work I needed to do. We are changed by our grief and should not become frightened by that change. Growth is surely taking place, and what we need to become will surface eventually. The most difficult part is allowing the growth to take place in its own way, without trying to direct it. Because I have always liked to be in control, either of myself or the world around me, I had a hard time with allowing things to be. It was alien to me. I was sure that if I didn't oversee everything, it would go to pot—a hands-off approach would end in chaos. To my surprise, not only didn't the world around me fall apart, but I started getting along with myself better. I didn't push so much or demand so much from myself. I stopped trying to control and began curiously to watch a new self emerge. Each grief brought a new lesson for me and a new step toward becoming the real person I always longed to be. The only explanation I can offer is that each person close to me had become very important. Consequently, I tried to be all the things each person wanted; I tried to be completely lovable and pleasing to all of them. At that time, I thought that was also what pleased me. After that role was interrupted and I could no longer play that part, I found that I could ease up on myself. I didn't have to try so hard. I could relax. I then became more liberated to be the person I was meant to be.

We do *not* have to go through the deaths of dearly loved people in order to grow. But, when we have a significant loss, we have the choice of either growing in the aftermath of that loss or becoming embittered and inflexible.

Enduring the Anniversaries

We will always experience moments of poignant memories. Special anniversaries or other significant dates will probably be the worst times. When we have these grief reactions after we thought our grief was over, we'll become frightened and disheartened. We will feel momentarily as if we have lost ground. So many bereaved people have said to me, in their own versions, "When I woke up on the morning of our wedding anniversary, I felt that sick, empty feeling again. My first reaction was to think it was starting all over again. I couldn't bear having to go through all that grief again. I think I would go off the deep end. It really scared me."

Anniversary reactions can pop up throughout our lifetime, surprising us when we least expect them. Even when we have consciously forgotten a special day, sometimes our unconscious hasn't, and the reactions will come without our least expectation. Or, we might find a memento that we didn't expect to turn up—a glove, a pipe in the bottom of a drawer, anything to remind us of something special about that beloved person. When we can learn that these sudden grief reactions are not permanent but will pass within a comparatively short time, we will not be so frightened by them.

Focusing

To make a new beginning, it is not enough only to center ourselves. Centering is an important first step because it helps us get in touch with our needs and potential. If we *only* center ourselves, we'll be trying to make our journey to new beginnings with old, worn-out baggage. We need new luggage adapted to our present needs. The focusing process, in which we turn again to the world outside our enclave of grief, selects some of our new luggage.

It is interesting how these two functions work together. Centering helps us know ourselves, but if we continue only to center, we might become self-centered, never fully able to take responsibility for our actions. On the other hand, if we use only focusing, we might be distracted by everyone else's ideas of who we should be and might stay compulsively busy. We would listen only to the outside world and never seek out our own needs and feelings.

Focusing provides an avenue for concentrating all our attention on one particular thing, thereby allowing us to put our new goals into action. By investing all our energy in a particular person or event, we are able to shut out the many distractions that keep us confused. We make decisions more quickly. We use our time more wisely. We budget our energy more efficiently. As a result, we successfully accomplish our goals.

To function as a new person and to develop a new or different life, we must employ *both* centering and focusing strategies. We must know more about our needs and wants by centering, but we must also put ourselves into motion by focusing on a course of action or a goal outside ourselves.

Keeping Loneliness in Perspective

Loneliness is a by-product of grief. Because grief makes us feel different from others, we naturally feel alienated from our world. "No one else could possibly feel as I do," we say. We are lonely for the companionship of that dearly beloved person and yearn to have him or her back again.

The return of that person isn't all we yearn for; we are caught up in secondary losses as well. If we have lost a spouse, we miss the comfort of marriage, of the couple way of life. If we have lost a child, we miss the forward motion a child provides us—the momentum of growth as well as the energy brought into the home by his or her presence. Our lives may now seem blunted and meaningless. If our parent has died, we will miss not being anyone's child any longer; we will have lost much of our personal history.

Loneliness is part of the transition of grief. We grieve over any and all the things we have lost. Endings force us into beginnings, but the slow middle part, that period when beginnings have not fully developed and we are still clinging to endings, is filled with loneliness.

When we can open ourselves to new people, places, ideas, and experiences, we expand to new horizons of hope. A word of caution, however: time and energy are needed to do this. We must be very gentle and patient with ourselves as we make this difficult transition.

Reaching Out

Reaching out is a sure cure for loneliness. Yet, it is probably one of the hardest tasks to undertake, especially after a major loss. Grief leaves us feeling insecure about ourselves and our world. We have a great fear that, because our beloved person has died and left us, others might do the same. It might be safer to trust no one, we think.

If we have made the decision to make a new life for ourselves, and if we feel that we have centered ourselves and know something of what we want, we need the energy and support of new friends to carry our decision through. For some of the people in the Tampa Study, support systems changed or fell away during the long period of bereavement. The death of a parent scarcely affected the lives of the bereaved's adult children, who had friends apart from the area of their original home. When a child died, many friends who were parents of the child's friends gradually drifted away; their common interest was gone. When a spouse died, the couple's companionate friends closed the circle, making the widow or widower feel like a "fifth wheel."

Mr. White stayed pretty much to himself for well over a year after his wife died. They had been married for forty years and he didn't even know how to go about reaching out, he said. Naturally, he was very lonely. In early December, I strongly recommended that he visit some family members in another part of the country; it seemed so sad to see him spend another Christmas alone. Reluctantly, he went to the local travel agency to buy his ticket. He recognized the woman who waited on him; he and his wife used to be in a bird-watching group with this woman. Mr. White soon learned that her husband had also died. It wasn't long before they were seeing each other and were finally married. Mr. White wondered why it had taken him so long to "reach out."

Hans Selye, the grandfather of stress research, tells us that, to combat stress, we need to develop "altruistic egotism"—we must earn our neighbors' love. He said that their love should be hoarded, saved up, to be used in times of stress. This is good advice. We need to learn to reach out to others, in order to build strong insurance against times when losses occur. When I asked the participants in the Tampa Study what was most important in helping them through grief, they overwhelmingly answered, "Friends, family, neighbors. Anyone who would take the time to listen." Fortunes are spent on life and health insurance each year, yet we often forfeit the one kind of insurance that will help in surviving a major loss: person insurance—hoarding our neighbors' love. The returns on that insurance can make all the difference in surviving a loss.

Understanding the Long Process of Grieving

How long does it take to get through the grieving process? Predicting how long it will take to move through the five phases of grief is like trying to predict how long it will take an adolescent to grow up. We can set a general time frame, but there will be variations because of personal differences. Some of us can complete the entire process in a month; others may require years. Much depends on our relationship to the one who has died, what our personalities are like, and the shock we experienced at the time of the death.

The phases can give us a general idea of what we will experience, but we simply cannot predict when we will complete a phase and move on to the next. Actually, there will be a great deal of overlap from one phase to another. We will have relapses, slipping back into the previous phase for a short while. Nothing in grief is ever smooth and predictable. It is a bumpy ride all the way.

ENDING THE RENEWAL PHASE

With renewal, your grief work is becoming complete. Take these actions for yourself and your future:

◆ Don't be afraid to continue talking about your
   beloved person, even though much time has

now passed since the death. You have every
right to include your memories as a healthy part
of your new life.

◆ Continue to maintain a health and physical fit-
ness regimen, eating well and exercising. You
will have more energy as you move out into a
new world that, hopefully, will become a way
of life.

◆ Realize that you have changed. Don't let others
try to put you back into old roles, and be especially aware of your own susceptibility to reen-
gaging them. This will take constant vigilance.
When you feel guilt over something you feel
you should do, be wary. This is a first sign that
pressure is being applied. Head it off quickly.

◆ Comb your consciousness for any unfinished
business you may not have completed with the
deceased. Now is the time to deal with it, either
in a small "homemade" ritual or by talking it
over with a trusted friend. Don't harbor unfinished sequences inside yourself.

◆ As you move into your newfound identity, allow personal restrictions to ease. If you worry,
"What will so-and-so think," do it anyhow. Feel
a sense of freedom as you do it. Being outra-
geous is fun sometimes.

◆ Plan a ritual to end your grief whenever you
feel ready. Instead of being anticlimactic after
this length of time, it is most appropriate. Few
rituals are offered for grief in the first place.
Devise your own. (Chapter 11 has some ideas.)

◆ Try to recount some of the gains that have
come to you during your bereavement—a newfound friend, development of more compassion for others, a new skill or interest. Tallying
the gains will help you to offset some of the
negative memories.

◆ Be aware of your new identity and don't be afraid to ask for what you need. You have a right to be your own person and to develop in any direction you choose.

◆ Remember that you have come through the worst thing that could ever happen, and you have survived. You faced the hardest kind of abandonment. After this, you need never fear the unknown again. You've been there and back.

◆ Be aware that anniversary reactions will sometimes catch you off guard. They pop up when you least expect them and may trigger a whole host of grief reactions. Don't be afraid: you are not relapsing.

◆ Begin to focus on your new goals. By doing this, you will learn the discipline necessary to put your desires into action and make them happen.

◆ Accept that you will feel lonely at times. Loneliness is part of the transition of grief. You will miss the roles you used to occupy and will long for things to be the same again. Acknowledge the loneliness until it passes.

◆ Reach out to others. This is one of the major requirements for establishing your new life. When you reach out, you offer comfort not only to yourself but to others as well. Thousands of people not far from you need the comfort of a friend. Reaching out can benefit mutually.

◆ Don't try to hurry the grief process or even think of it in terms of time limits. You will move through as you can. Putting pressure on yourself will only make your grief worse.

Flight

Dawn suddenly stirs me. I feel the knife-like early
mourning pain. Then, in sleepy reverie, I remember.
        He is gone.

First-wakening aching memories are interrupted by the
flapping, chirping sound on the sill outside. I listen.
        I hear his voice.

Below the sheet is the familiar searing pain similar
to the pain of birth I gave to him.
Slowly, the inrush of strength moves me from the covers
to the window.
I listen.

My new winged friends are singing the tune becoming
more gracious to the senses   —   "Flight."
The black feathers expectantly flutter in short sequence.

The rapid, ritual daily flight occurs once more.

Mary Howren Howerton

7

When a Child Dies— Parental Bereavement

It's the worst possible thing that could ever happen. My little girl . . . she hadn't even been here that long. My God . . . it is too soon for her to die. She was supposed to have gone to college, marry, have children . . . my grandchildren. She wasn't supposed to die first. She should have buried me first, not the other way around.

Bereaved mother, age 34

The death of a child is the most severe and the longest lasting of all griefs. It has rightly been described as the "ultimate tragedy." When we lose a child, it is like having part of ourselves sliced away. The raw, open wound is slow to close. Repeated infections delay the healing. New wounds are constantly inflicted on the old one by secondary losses connected to the child's death. The pain is unbearable. Even when scar tissue has formed, the agony of living without that part of ourselves leaves us feeling isolated and different, awkward and unsure. There is no prosthesis. Slowly, we become aware that we must somehow learn to live with our worst loss.

After Jim was killed, a number of people said to me, "You are so strong. If my child died, I don't think I could ever live through it." This used to make me angry. I thought, "What choice do I have? I have to put one foot in front of the other and keep going." Unless we are actively suicidal, we really don't have a choice but to keep on "keeping on." I use the term "actively suicidal" because I believe that most people who have lost a child reach a point, during their grief, when they wouldn't care whether something happened to them or not. (They would then be out of their awful pain.) Yet, most would not actively try to do something to harm themselves.

WHAT CAUSES PARENTAL BEREAVEMENT TO BE SO SEVERE?

Child Death Is Rare

Why is the death of a child such an unbearable sorrow? Why does this type of death shock us so profoundly? We lack the experience to deal with it. There is no time to practice. When it happens, the shock runs deep. We don't know how to behave, how to react, how to survive. Because child death is such a relatively rare occurrence in our society, we have little expectation that it will ever happen to us.

A hundred years ago, more children died than older people. There were serious contagious diseases to reckon with, and the health codes we have today didn't exist. With modern preventive medicine, the trend became reversed. People continue to die, but they don't often die young.

The Strength of the Parent–Child Bond

No relationship is more important than the attachment between ourselves and our children. The connection is more than one of blood; deep emotional ties bind us to our children throughout life. My children were love objects; they had a strong unifying effect between my husband and myself. Our children connected us to each other deeply and completely. We felt our oneness through our children.

The parent–child bond begins in our fantasies during pregnancy. We try to picture what the newborn will look like, be like, or do. As mothers, we are aware of the growing fetus; as it begins to move, our fantasies intensify. The naming of the baby, the sharing of our fantasies with our husbands, and the presence of a new personality become more exciting, and the bonding grows daily. With the birth of the baby, the bonding with the father begins. As they care for the infant together, the parents' sharing reaches a deeper level than before. Ambivalent feelings arise from time to time. The parents might feel resentment if they become tired and burdened, particularly after several sleepless nights. Strangely enough, the more difficult the situation, the stronger the parent–child bond grows, and the more there is a need to protect and take responsibility for this new little creature.

We Identify with Our Children

As our child begins to become more responsive to us, our delight in him or her grows. There is such a special joy in having our child greet us with a big smile, with arms thrown out to be loved. We observe each accomplishment with pride. We begin to see ourselves in our child and to project our future to match our child's. In essence, our child becomes our future.

Because our children are our own flesh and blood, we begin to see ourselves in them almost from the very beginning: their eyes, features, bodily contours, hair, gender. Stepchildren or adopted children pick up our mannerisms. We begin to see ourselves even in these children. The childhood years become a reliving of our own childhood. As our child grows, so does our own involvement. We see both our positive and negative characteristics developing in our child. Our child is our mirror, in many ways.

When our child dies, we mourn not only for the deprivation of the child's presence, but also for the lost aspects of ourselves. When we have to learn to survive with only a part of ourselves remaining, it is like learning to walk after one leg has been amputated. This is why the death of a child has been described as an invisible "phantom limb" agony. We remain physically intact but we are emotionally fragmented; our sense of self has been badly mutilated. This is a loss with no prosthesis.

Children Are Our Future

Besides the hopes, dreams, and expectations that surround each child's birth, our future is carried forth in the genes that protect the lineage of our family. George, a young father in the Tampa Study, talked of his feelings about heritage:

> It's like leaving a piece of yourself behind or something. Like the only thing. People don't make their mark on the world, right? Not everybody becomes famous, not everybody has a book or something that people will read after they're gone. But children are a surefire way of leaving a piece of yourself behind. I won't have that now.

When a child dies, we feel that our immortality has been stolen, our future interrupted.

Children as Social Agents

Our children are like a rite of passage for us, a coming of age. We are grown-ups when we have children. The community accepts us as adults and gives us the rank of responsible people.

Children bring us social contacts, through their activities, schools, and different events. As such, our children become a focal point for making family plans, and a major source of security and happiness for us. When we move to a new community, we often make social connections through our children's friends and their families.

When a child dies, we lose the connection our child gave us with the world. A special child is no longer here to radiate energy and enthusiasm. We begin to realize how much we depended on our child's activities to keep us involved.

WHAT MAKES PARENTAL GRIEF DIFFERENT FROM ALL OTHER LOSSES?

Despair

The reason parental grief is so different from other losses has to do with excess. Because loss of a child is such an unthinkable loss, everything is intensified, exaggerated, and lengthened. Guilt and anger are almost always present in every significant loss, but these emotions are inordinate with grieving parents. Experts estimate that it takes anywhere from three to five years to reach renewal after a spouse dies, but parental grief might go on for ten to twenty years or maybe a lifetime. Our lives are so severely altered when our child dies that there can be no replacements. Substitutes offer little respite. This is not to say that there is no hope for happiness. It is just that the shock and severity of this kind of loss leaves us feeling completely helpless and full of dark despair.

I remember trying to face the reality of Jim's death months after the accident. The thought would come to me suddenly in a nightmarish revelation, "My son is dead. Oh God. Jim's gone forever." That would usually be as far as I could get. That thought would be quickly followed with an agonizing cry, "Oh no! It's not true," and I would fall into paroxysms of racking sobs, the grief too painful to even put into words.

When I talked with bereaved parents in the Tampa Study, they looked as if they had had the wind knocked out of them; they were leaden and devoid of strength; their will to fight was gone. Whether the death was caused by illness or accident made no difference. The age of the child didn't matter. The impossibility of surviving their child left them shattered. Life made no sense. "Why?" was an obsessive rumination with no answers. Through my own experience, I knew something of what they felt. It was a raw, visible torment.

Confusion

If your child has died, you may wonder why you are having such a hard time concentrating on anything. Even the simplest of tasks is almost too much to figure out. Concentration is difficult after most losses, but, when a child dies, the parents find it impossible to focus. There is a jumble of unintelligible thoughts as the mind races desperately to take in the horrible tragedy. Even our usual distractions, such as light reading or watching TV, no longer can offer the escape they used to. Our minds simply can't slow down long enough to quiet our confusion.

Jennifer had planned for her new baby even before she got pregnant. After she knew for sure that she would have her baby in July, she and her husband, Michael, began preparing for the arrival. They painted and decorated the nursery. They bought some new furniture, a crib, and a changing table. They shopped for several weeks for an antique dresser and rocking chair that they could refinish themselves. By the time the baby was due, everything was ready. It was as perfect as they could make it, and Jennifer was delighted.

Delivery went well and after only five hours of labor, Jennifer and Michael had a beautiful five-and-a-half-pound boy. In the second day of life, the baby began to have pulmonary problems. He was put on oxygen. When his condition worsened, he was moved to the intensive care unit. He died on the third day, with Michael and Jennifer beside him. They had not even been able to hold him while he was alive.

Jennifer's parents lived in the same city so, rather than go home, she stayed with them for a couple of weeks to recuperate. She talked with me about how difficult it was to make decisions:

> I found that making decisions was for me extremely difficult. Normally, decisions are very simple and easy to do, something I don't think about. But now a decision of what to do tomorrow even was a trauma. And they would explain it to me how this is very common, and they said that you do one thing at a time and then you build up to your normal activity. But we were going to come back to our house, so I said, "OK, let's go back on Thursday." Well, it was such a trauma for me to actually try and plan how I am going to pack up my clothes, how I am going to put things in the bathroom in a box to get them back. I mean, these are normal things that wouldn't bother anybody, but for me it was just too hard. It was like the most difficult thing that I had ever tackled in my life. I couldn't.
>
> So I finally got myself worked up to such a tizzy over just moving, I said to Michael, "I can't do it." So we took another ten days, and then it was better.

Our constant preoccupation with our lost child makes concentrating on anything impossible. Our habitual tasks now require careful forethought. Before the death, there were things we usually did without thinking about them— making the bed, straightening the kitchen, cooking. But after such a loss, simply preparing breakfast can be an impossible task. Jeannie, a forty-three-year-old wife and mother, described her dilemma in the kitchen after one of her three children died:

> I try to get up in the morning to fix breakfast for everyone. I stumble around in the kitchen, open the refrigerator and my mind goes blank. Off hand, I can't even tell you what goes with what. It is almost as if I'm in someone else's kitchen. Most of the time I go back to bed in utter despair.

Anger

We cannot be passive and accepting when the worst thing in the world has happened. We're helpless in the face of everything. There is no rational way to deal with our child's death. The very order of the universe has been altered. We have nothing, no guidelines or direction, to prepare us for this tragedy. We must make up our lives as we go along.

Because we have accepted the responsibility for our child and have been there to solve his or her problems and offer comfort and nurturance, we are now left with empty hands and a feeling of total powerlessness. There is nothing we can do to solve this problem. It has been taken out of our hands. No matter what we do, promise, or say, we can't bring our child back.

People in the Tampa Study verbalized anger directed toward the health care team. Many felt that more could have been done by the doctor, the hospital staff, the rescue team, and anyone who was involved in the events surrounding the death. One mother, whose adult son had died of internal injuries during a hospital stay, thought that he might have fallen out of bed and that the hospital staff was covering it up. A father was justifiably angry because his son's murderer had not been apprehended. He felt that, because he had little clout, he was getting the runaround by the police department. He was afraid that the murderer would never get caught and he worried about that possibility all the time. His wife had mixed feelings about convicting anyone. She felt that the murderer should be put away to protect society, but she wasn't sure that she really wanted to know who did it. The vindication would not bring her son back and would only intensify her hate. The helplessness brought about by losing their son in such a senseless and violent manner was overwhelming.

Another major source of anger for bereaved parents in the Tampa Study was the way in which they were told of their child's death—usually by health care personnel. Delivering this news is an awful job for anyone, but it is sometimes made worse when those selected to do the telling do it in a brusque or awkward manner. Mr. and Mrs. Bellini had been called to their city's large hospital in the middle of the night because their son had been hurt in a car accident. Mrs. Bellini later told me:

> They didn't tell us when we came in; we sat there for over an hour. Nobody came in, and finally my husband went out and asked if they couldn't please tell us something. They said the doctor is busy right now and he will be with you in a few minutes. And then I kind of got hope. I thought, well maybe it wasn't Bobby. Finally, this doctor came in and he said, "I didn't see your son. The doctor that saw him has left. But," he said, "he is dead," like that.

The doctor then left the Bellinis in the care of a nurse, who gave them a small package of their son's clothing along with one sleeping pill each for themselves. We can only imagine the bitterness that Mr. and Mrs. Bellini felt at having this heartbreaking news given to them in such a cold and secondhand manner.

Our anger is a means of giving expression to the powerlessness we feel when our child dies. We are incapable of changing even the smallest detail about this death, now that it has happened. Still, we rage at the senselessness of the tragedy. We were the ones who were supposed to care for this child. Because we had taken on the responsibility of protection, we believe we were somehow the ones who failed. We become very angry and project our anger on anyone or anything that we can. We give ourselves a large share of blame.

Anger is best dealt with by talking it out with a trusted friend—someone who will accept the anger and listen to our railing over and over until we have worked it out of our systems. Anger is the most normal of responses at a time like this. To distract ourselves from it means that we stuff it down inside us, only to have it fume up again and again.

Guilt Is Inevitable

Guilt is a by-product of grief. No matter what the loss, or how, when, or where it happened, we are usually plagued with remembrances of things we shouldn't have done or said, or things we wish we had done or said. It takes a while to work through these feelings of remorse, to finally reassure ourselves that we did all we could, given the circumstances. We continually forget the advantage that hindsight offers.

With the death of a child, guilt is doubly pronounced. Because we feel responsible for our children, when something happens to them we immediately blame ourselves. If we or they had been more on guard, the death would never have happened. Granted, these are irrational feelings, but they are part of the "if only" ruminations of bereaved parents: if only I had come home a few minutes earlier; if only I had refused him the car; if only I had not waited so long to get help; if only . . . , if only . . . . These circulating broodings are obsessive, leaving us to deal only with the empty "Why?"

Guilt will continue to torture us until we are willing to forgive ourselves, as well as others, for this unbearable tragedy. We need to heal our pain, yet we resist the healing measures. We fear letting go of our grief because it is akin to letting go of our child. If we have nothing else left of him or her, we still have our pain as a connection.

It took me ten years to see the importance of letting go of the guilt. I had carried dark and painful thoughts of the things I could have done to have made my son's life happier. I blanked out the need for discipline and for teaching responsibility and self-reliance. I could only remember the times I had said "No." Much later, a small group of six bereaved parents got together to share their loss reactions, and within this group I began to allow my shadowy thoughts and feelings to come slowly to the surface. As I was able to share them one by one, I found the burden of guilt growing lighter and forgiveness beginning to gain some strength. I struggled at first, and held back, fearing the reactions of others and my own reactions to myself. As I grew stronger, the fear lessened and I was able to focus more on the joys my son had brought to my world.

Stress

Parental grief carries more stress than other types of loss because the shock phase lasts much longer and the secondary losses are more numerous. In the Tampa Study, more physical problems and symptoms were reported by bereaved parents than by bereaved people who had survived the death of a spouse or a parent.

Grief uses enormous quantities of psychic energy, and it is the ever draining aspect of this debilitating outlay that keeps us off balance during bereavement. As I described in Chapter 3, the prolonged nature of the stress response creates the greatest difficulty. Physically, we are doing the equivalent work of hard labor, without realizing it. We are bone-weary at times, but our high level of adrenaline output keeps us constantly moving about. The effects of our inordinate fatigue and stress create irritability. The lack of joy in our daily existence reflects our heaviness. We are fearful that our lives will always be like this—joyless, lacking in meaning or goals.

George, a forty-one-year-old bereaved father, lost his only son to leukemia when the boy was only fifteen. He struggled with the anguish of this loss and experienced shock after shock as he tried to make real the awful tragedy:

> I know if I dwell on his death, I can talk to anybody about it in general, like "Yeh, my son died of leukemia." Things like that . . . in that way . . . and I don't notice it, but if I start dwelling on it in my mind, about his death, the time he was in the hospital, and right up to the point where I'm sure he knew he was dying, then the fear comes over me. I almost can feel like I'm going into shock, it's that severe. And I just have to block it out of my mind.

I relive it, as I say, if I dwell on it. I relive all those scenes at the hospital and I get to thinking what was going through his mind because I'm sure he knew that he was dying. So I can feel it come on, it just feels like a . . . fear and I guess it's the fear of dying. And I'm sure he feared it and that really affects me physically.

Every time George put up a mental block to his fears, he created another stressful situation later on, when the thoughts gained access again to his consciousness.

This type of thinking goes on every day for bereaved parents, until they are exhausted and weakened. It has been found that the grief of parents seems to build and grow worse in the third year after their child's death. This is why it is so important to get the rest we need while we are trying to heal. Because of the long haul of grief, it is essential to begin to take care of our health in every way possible.

EFFECTS ON THE MARRIAGE

Marital Problems

All kinds of rough estimates have been made as to the impact that the death of a child has on a marriage. Some studies have estimated that as high as ninety percent of all couples have problems in their marriage within the first two years after losing a child. If we are talking of problems now and not divorce, I would say that nearly 100 percent of all couples who are mourning a child have some problems now and then. Most marriages have some problems just dealing with the simple and ordinary things in life, during bereavement for a child.

Divorce is quite another thing. It is very difficult to ascertain an estimate of the divorce rate following a child's death, because we don't have studies that have lasted long enough to give any accurate figures. No one in the Tampa Study divorced, but almost all the parents had some difficulty.

Much of the difficulty lies in the couples' perception that each partner can always lean on the other partner when either feels insecure or upset. As parents, we live in a "together" society. We worked together during labor. We had our baby. We shared the sleepless infant years. We watched together as our baby took first steps. At each developmental stage, we celebrated our child's advance.

Now what do we do? We are alone in our grief at the most painful time of our lives. Each of us is too burdened to carry the other. We are on our own. Instead of a grieving couple, we have become two bereaved individuals.

After Jim's death, Hersh and I withdrew from each other. We closed up in our separate corners. We hardly spoke. I was furious with him. Among other things, I blamed him for having been too strict a father and never sharing time with Jim. He blamed me for blaming him. We were too crushed to understand any of it. Hersh was trying to be the strong one. Because he hadn't cried, I accused him of not loving Jim. I had no way of knowing that I had displaced all my anger at Jim's death onto Hersh. Because display of anger had never been allowed in my family of origin, my only response was to withdraw. It became *my* grief. I wouldn't let anyone in.

Looking back on that period, I wish we had had a moderator to help us communicate with each other. If we had had the benefit of a group like Compassionate Friends, I believe we could have eventually worked through our separateness. Instead, we stumbled on in our marriage, never really feeling our "partnership" again.

We eventually formed a Compassionate Friends group and we kept up the façade of a couple, but we could never recapture the full depth of trust that had given us our strength together. We became one of the divorce fatalities. We always loved each other and remained close friends, but we were never able to bridge the chasm of hurt we inflicted on each other during those first years after Jim died.

Each parent grieves differently. A mother and a father may not suffer the same loss when their child dies. Each had a separate and unique relationship and will grieve for different things. The process will not move at the same speed for both of them. The father's grief may be diminishing while the mother's grief remains the same or grows more acute. Unless each parent is quite attuned to the other, this difference in grieving will be interpreted as another sign of either overemotional reacting or not caring enough. This is one time when it is important to balance emotions by meeting with a trustworthy group and sharing some of the confusion that comes with trying to match a spouse's pace in the grief process.

Grief of Fathers

Men and women have their separate roles in all cultures, and ours is no exception. These roles complement each other when things are going well. When things aren't going well, however, these separate roles act to make communication difficult. In our society, a man is socialized to take the following roles:

Being strong—a macho man who controls his emotions;

Competing, winning in a crisis, and being the best;

Protecting the family and its possessions;

Being the family provider;

Being the problem solver—fixing things;

Controlling actions within the family and the environment;

Being self-sufficient—standing on his own two feet.

When men are socialized to be strong, controlling, self-sufficient family protectors, the problem is that these characteristics work against open expression of emotions, grief included. Emotional displays are often seen as weaknesses. When a child dies, events are out of a father's control.

Besides feeling an inner agony that he can't express, he feels powerless, stripped of his sense of self. He is angry and guilty, and has a strong sense of personal failure.

When the father remains woodenly stoic, trying to be all the things that are expected of him, he gives the impression of one who has no grief. When he doesn't want to talk about the child, the mother takes this as further indication that he simply doesn't care.

Grief of Mothers

A mother is socialized to fill different roles. She is expected to be the nurturer, the caregiver, the hub of the family, to communicate with each member and help the members communicate with each other. She is used to carrying the emotional burden of the family. For the most part, women have been socialized to believe that it is their place to create the family circle. When a child dies, the circle is broken. Grief freezes the mother into a shell, and she cannot function in her prescribed roles as she once did. She grieves not only for her child, but also for the loss of the delicate balance in the family system.

Because she needs more nurturance for herself and is less able to give nurturance to others, she turns to her husband for help. But she often finds him withdrawn and unable to communicate. This is naturally seen as lack of love for the child—or worse, for her. Because of greater sensitivity in grief than at any other time in life, the hurts are pushed down deeper and deeper. There is no way of dislodging or deflecting them.

Even sexual expression, which helped draw the couple together in the past, is impeded by the inability to trust or feel close now.

As a result, mothers find themselves locked in social isolation, not able to understand the full implications of what is taking place but having strong needs of their own that go unfulfilled.

FINDING MEANING IN THE LOSS

Shortly after Jim died, if anyone had asked me about any meaning in his death, I would have been probably too stunned to answer. The loss was incomprehensible to me. How could I find meaning of any sort in what had happened? The fresh sorrow was as much as I could deal with, and survival seemed more than I could manage. There were days when I was convinced I wouldn't make it.

However, as I continued into the first few months, I became aware of a small, persistent hope deep within me. Out of the depths of my loss emerged a desire to reach out to others whose child had died. I watched the papers. One day, I read of a fourteen-year-old boy who had been killed on his bicycle as he delivered the afternoon newspaper. That day, I baked a cake and took it to his home. I gasped when I saw the broken bike leaning against the side of the garage. I almost turned away, tears beginning to flood my eyes. But I made myself go to the door. When I rang the bell, the door was opened by a young woman whose eyes were blurred from recent tears. It was an awkward moment for me; I was afraid that I might be intruding. But she was kind enough to invite me in and ask me to sit.

I wish I could say that I had just the right words to make her feel better, but I'm afraid I was not too articulate. Looking back, I understand that it didn't matter very much what I said. She seemed glad that I was there. We cried together and I left shortly after. Later, I received a note from her:

Dear Catherine,

You were so thoughtful to take the time to visit me. I can't tell you how much I appreciated it. None of my neighbors have come close to me and I can only guess that they don't know what to say. But you know, it really isn't important what people say. Just caring, just acknowledging my loss, is all I really need.

You made a big difference. Thanks.

We may never find a reason for our child's death, but, if we work at it, we can begin to make some meaning from the loss. Whenever we extend a kindness to someone who needs us, we are putting meaning into life. Forming a closer tie with our higher power through prayer and meditation creates spiritual meaning. Donating time and energy to a worthy cause, or helping with a group such as Compassionate Friends, MADD (Mothers Against Drunk Drivers), or SHARE (Source of Help in Airing and Resolving Experiences), we begin to put meaning back into our lives.

Grief is a long and difficult journey full of treacherous ruts and bumpy potholes. We do make it to peace and joy eventually; I can vouch for that. Along the way, we will meet friends who help us and friends whom we will help. These experiences add a new richness to our lives that we never thought would be possible again. These friends will put meaning back into our lives and finally help us discover the meaning in our loss. I can vouch for that as well.

Ours and Mine

Give me your hand.
I will take you a walk
In my yard
Which once was ours.

Here is where the melons grew.
I did not plant them,
They were the work of God.
They came up running
From the compost heap
And fell exhausted
Way out here.
In time they grew puffed up with pride
At their achievement.

These sprawling trellised morning glories,
White, blue, and pink,
I did not plant them,
They were hiding to surprise Sally,
But they were too late.
Even so, their little trumpets
Go tooting hope to the sun,
Rain or shine.

These rocks and cactuses,
A yellow bombardment in their season,
Now overgrown with weeds
Like yonder flower garden,
Like my life.

Now you are tired.
Another day
I will take your hand
And show you other wonders
In my yard
Which once was ours.

Harold Boysen

8

Death of a Spouse—Losing a Mate

When my husband died, I don't really remember too much about it. As I said, the boys seemed to think that I went into a state of shock. I don't know—for four or five days, I didn't know who I was or where I was. I didn't know anybody. As a matter of fact, my closest friend came to see me and I didn't even know her. But when I came out of it and realized what had happened, I really felt awful. It really hit me then, especially when my sons came in and started talking to me—that this was the way it had to be, that this was the way it was.

Widow, age 64

Mrs. Collins's husband, age 70, had died suddenly of a heart attack. Several months before, Mr. Collins somehow had had a feeling of impending trouble. He had often tried to talk to his wife about his death: what she should do when it happened, and how she should take care of herself. Mrs. Collins firmly avoided any talk of death, believing that he would always be around. Besides, she always thought that she would die first.

Mr. Collins had always done *everything* for his wife. She was totally dependent on him to do things around the house and to organize her life for her. She said later:

After he died, I didn't like being alone, especially after he had done so much for me, and even my sons tried to explain the same thing. "Mother, Dad wanted to teach you all of this and you wouldn't listen. Now you have to do all of this and you have to do it by yourself, you have to learn how." Which was true. So afterwards, I didn't have anybody to blame but myself because he really did, he did everything. But I have tried. I have done a lot of things that I have never done before for myself. I have tried and I found out that if I keep at it long enough, I learn . . . but it is still a hard time to have to learn.

BREAKING THE CONNECTIONS

Some of us lean on our mates more than others do. We don't mean to lean, but our marriage shapes up that way, just gradually becoming more one-sided. When this happens, bereavement for our mate is much more difficult. Not only must we suffer the agony of separation anxiety, but our feelings of deprivation become even greater. We must struggle through the frustration of trying to learn new things when our concentration and stress tolerance are at their lowest ebb.

Men are equally prone to becoming emotionally dependent on their wives and creating the same lonely suffering for themselves. Emotional dependence leaves us feeling empty, abandoned, and frustrated by our futile efforts to find ways to fill the void.

The Broken Heart

A broken heart is not a myth. There is firm documentation regarding this devastating effect on some people who experience a significant loss. When we lose our mate, the person we have relied on for support, the one we have depended on in countless ways, is no longer there. The partnership is dissolved; half of us is gone.

The thought of losing our mate is so dreadful that we tend to put the possibility out of our minds. Some of us fear that to talk about death with our mate may bring it on. Some of us are leery about ever signing a living will—or drawing any sort of will. Others even hesitate to buy life insurance because we seem to be betting with the company on when we are going to die. "To enter into a contract like that," the superstitious say, "is to invite trouble."

Few couples die together. Widowhood is the inevitable conclusion of all marriages that don't end in divorce. We are rarely prepared to lose our mate, and denial appears to be our only defense against the potential suffering we envision.

The Stress of Grief

We probably know more about spousal bereavement than any other type of loss, because most of the research on bereavement has studied the death of a mate. It has even been listed on a popular stress test as the number-one stressor among all losses. There is no question that the death of a spouse represents one of the most intense stresses that we can live through.

As early as 1940, one of the first major research projects on bereavement was underway. This was a study initiated by the tragic Coconut Grove Nightclub fire in Boston. The fire, which quickly enveloped the entire nightclub, trapped hundreds of people as they jammed the two exits and tried to escape. There were countless deaths. Some husbands and wives were separated by the press of the panicked crowd. Some escaped and others were trapped and killed. The fire was one of the worst disasters to happen in this country, and the grief was overwhelming. Survivors were inconsolable; many who had lost their spouses found it hard to understand how they could escape and their mate could be killed.

Erich Lindemann, a physician at Massachusetts General Hospital, was able to set up a clinic for the survivors of this horrible tragedy. Their grief provided much early information regarding the symptoms that are suffered during bereavement.

We know much more now. We know that there is a significant incidence of illness, accidents, and even deaths among bereaved people.

We usually think of grief as affecting only our emotions, but there are always physical effects of one kind or another because it is impossible to separate the mind from the body. We might suffer headaches, gastrointestinal problems, weight loss, sleep loss, fatigue, and similar symptoms. More serious illnesses can occur as our alarm system works overtime to keep us alert and on guard.

Because grief work is just as draining as physical labor, we must use great quantities of energy just to get through each day. Consequently, our resistance is lowered and we have increased vulnerability to all types of illnesses. With a heavy expenditure of energy over several months, a high rate of illnesses and death occurs among bereaved people. We must pay careful attention to our health, particularly during the first year after the death. Proper rest, good diet, routine exercise, and a physical examination by a doctor will help to ensure good health during bereavement.

Low Income

When we are deprived of our mate's presence; when we have to take over the jobs he or she did in addition to our own; when we are left to raise children alone; when all these factors weigh heavily on our shoulders and we are the sole economic source for a family, we find that the stress of grief is more than anyone can deal with. Low income adds immeasurably to the difficulty of surviving a spouse. For many wives who have never held a job outside the home, the insecurity is even more frightening. They must now seek employment at a time when their self-confidence is at its lowest. For husbands who have children to raise, there is the worry of how to pay for their care and the guilt of not spending enough time with them. Deep financial worry is an added burden on the grieving widow or widower.

Women seem to suffer more because of a lack of work availability and job preparedness. There are more high-salaried jobs for men, and men are usually better prepared to handle a broader range of marketable tasks. Widows, especially those with young children, must often rely solely on public agencies to carry the family financially.

WHAT MARRIAGE MEANS

Creating Bonds

Rarely do we hear of parents arranging marriages anymore. In our culture, we choose our own mates. They often become our best friends and companions. The trend to smaller nuclear families promotes close friendships between spouses. When we live far from our extended families, we rely on our immediate family to provide everything we need—a large order and a huge responsibility to place on any marriage.

Role Expectations

Even when marriages are far from perfect and are based only on superficial need exchange, important bonds are established. These bonds are based on the role expectations between the mates. For example, traditionally, the wife offers nurturance and emotional care while the husband provides for and protects the family. Within these major areas lie many separate tasks that each mate expects of the other. These role requirements generally are well-established within the first year of marriage and are usually taken for granted in a fairly short time.

When Bonds Are Broken

When one of the partners dies, the survivor not only loses all the emotional support, friendship, and companionship, but must find some way to fulfill all of the family's tasks and responsibilities. Finding others to fill these roles, or trying to perform them oneself, alone and unsupported, is overwhelming. Faced with all these interlocking factors, it's hard to know what is really being grieved. Grief becomes a conglomerate of deprivations and responsibilities rather than only a physical separation (which is painful enough). When we lose a mate, we lose part of our physical self, part of our social self, and an enormous part of our emotional self. It takes several years to renew those parts and have them function normally.

WHAT SEPARATION MEANS

Eating Alone

Eating alone seems to sum up the deprivation of spousal bereavement. Helen, recently widowed at thirty-four, told me that she had lost twenty pounds in three months after her husband died. She felt it was partly due to the fact that she could not bear to sit down at the table alone. John, a widower, told me of eating at the kitchen counter or at the refrigerator, taking things out absentmindedly without an appetite. When he fixed a tray to eat before the TV, he had poignant memories of when he and Suzanne had done that together. It always made him cry, so he avoided it.

Quantities at most stores are not packaged for one serving, and it is hard to cook a single helping. "When your appetite is nil, why bother?" was the attitude of many people in the Tampa Study who were trying not to feel too lonely while at home alone. The widowers ate out or were invited to dinner more often than the widows. This situation, unfortunately, seems to be prevalent in most areas of the country. Those who were able to avoid eating alone all the time nevertheless dreaded it when they had to eat alone again.

Sleeping Alone

Not having a sexual partner seems to be less of a deprivation for bereaved spouses than sleeping alone. After becoming used to having someone in bed beside us, the empty place feels hollow and cold. Waking in the middle of the night to find ourselves huddled alone in one corner of the bed is a nightmare. Getting up in the morning with no one to say good morning to takes the meaning out of the day.

After six months of being a widow, Mildred said that she longed to be held again by someone who really cared for her. That type of nurturance was missed more than sex at the beginning of her bereavement. At a time when we don't feel very safe in the world, tender arms are a satisfying comfort. We value the little things that weave together the richness of our relationship. When they are taken away, they subtract the color from our life scene.

Caring for Children Alone

Lanine was left with six small children, including a set of twins, when her husband, Grant, was killed in a car wreck. The children's ages ranged from twelve to two years. Grant had always been a wonderful help in sharing the care of the children—the baths, the meals, even the laundry. The one area where he was always needed was discipline of the children. Lanine didn't seem to carry weight with the two older boys; she was unable to firmly control them. They were "a handful," she told me. Six weeks after Grant's accident, Lanine was still in shock. Her parents had been able to stay for a while to help, but they were now getting ready to go back to their home in Ohio. Lanine couldn't bear to think of their leaving. She was scared of dealing with everything alone.

After her folks left, she tried to manage with some day help for the baby—the rest of the children were in school—but things quickly fell apart. The two older boys began acting out both at school and at home. To control them, Lanine began buying them things. She put in a swimming pool. She bought expensive camping gear and took them all away for a weekend camping trip. After only one night, she packed them all up and came home. It was too much for her. The kids had run all over the camp.

The school counselor recommended therapy for the three older children, but Lanine was furious and responded that her children weren't crazy.

As the conditions at home grew worse, Lanine began to drink "just to calm my nerves." Things went from bad to worse, and eventually the children were taken away from Lanine. She was sent to an alcohol treatment center for an extended period of time.

I lost track of the family and its heartbreaking situation. This family had somehow slipped through the cracks until it was too late for anyone to help them. Lanine wasn't prepared to deal with her large family alone. Grant had been the strong one and, without him there, Lanine did not have enough personal resources to hold everything together. The children's grief was never acknowledged, and Lanine remained in shock and denial for many months.

Nancy handled her situation in a different way. When Richard was ill in the hospital, she prepared her children for his death by explaining carefully the medical condition of their father. The two older children were able to visit their father in the hospital and tell him they loved him, something that helped them later on. On the day he died, Nancy had discussed his condition with them and had told them that he would probably die soon. During the services, Nancy made sure that they understood what was going on and each was allowed to express grief in some way. After the funeral, Nancy overheard someone saying to her oldest boy that he was now "the man of the house" and would have to "take over." This upset Nancy, who promptly took the boy aside and told him to take those comments with a grain of salt because people just didn't know what else to say.

Nancy later gathered her children around her and told them that they needed to share this loss together. They began doing things together as a family, without the usual divisions that the death of a parent causes. They grieved for their father but, by *sharing* the grief with each other, their burden was lightened.

Nancy told me that one of the hardest things she had to do was accompany the boys to Little League, where their father had always been active. On the first night, after the boys' team won, one little player presented her with a ball signed by all the players. She had been fairly stoic until then, but the presentation caused her to break down. Still, she wouldn't have missed that moment for anything.

Loneliness and Deprivation

Loneliness is a major problem for bereaved spouses. How can we escape loneliness when part of us is gone and no replacement is in sight? We live in an increasingly couple-companionate culture. Although there are many new singles groups, it is difficult to fit in when we have recently been part of a couple. This takes a lot of "getting used to"; it doesn't happen overnight. Besides, a new life takes more energy than we may have right now.

The bereaved spouses in the Tampa Study were no exception to the loneliness problem. Margaret Callahan lives on a beautiful Florida lake that would seem like heaven to a honeymoon couple. But her husband died a few months ago, and she is now totally isolated out there, with few callers. The couple hadn't been able to maintain many close friends during Mr. Callahan's last illness, and people have stopped even calling on the phone.

This was a third marriage for Mrs. Callahan. Her first husband died of a massive heart attack when she was forty-two, leaving her with two daughters to raise. After several years, she remarried, but discovered that her new husband was an alcoholic. After four difficult years, she divorced him, vowing she would stay single from then on.

Instead, she met Mr. Callahan, a widower. They realized that they had much in common and enjoyed each other. After several months, they were married. Mrs. Callahan was fifty-two, Mr. Callahan was seventy-two. It was a good marriage. They traveled, fished, and enjoyed friends together, until he became ill.

After a diagnosis of cancer of the liver, he was hospitalized twice and had spent his last year in a great deal of pain. When the doctors felt they could do no more, they suggested that he either go home or be put in a nursing home. Mrs. Callahan brought him home, rented a wheelchair and a hospital bed, and cared for him herself. She lifted him in and out of bed, which was hard for her. She seemed glad to do anything that would allow him to stay at home. He ate fairly well and enjoyed his meals.

At the table one evening, he suddenly stiffened and remained that way for a minute or two. Later, Mrs. Callahan was told that he had suffered a stroke. After that, things got much worse. He had a hard time swallowing and refused solid food. Mrs. Callahan had to painstakingly strain all his food. Taking care of him took every minute of her time.

When his kidneys blocked, he was rushed to the hospital in severe pain and placed in intensive care. After previously being with him every minute, Mrs. Callahan could see him for only a few minutes each hour. She was troubled by the many tubes and machines around him but was more upset that she could no longer be his caregiver.

The morning he died, his birthday, he was conscious and knew what day it was. Mrs. Callahan was told that his alertness was a good sign. It was suggested that she take a break and go to the coffee shop for a while. When she came back to the room after only forty-five minutes, Mr. Callahan had died. After all the time she had spent caring for him and loving him, she was not with him when he died. As she told it:

> About twenty minutes after I was there, they said, "Why don't you go get a cup of coffee." That was about noon. I said I didn't want any. They said, "Well, we think that you should go out . . . get some coffee or something and come back after a while." . . . They kept insisting, so finally I did go. And when I came back he was gone, dead. And I think they knew he was going. They didn't want me in there.
>
> Before I went for coffee, he was still conscious, I could see. He kind of closed his eyes like he was resting or something. He could hear me. They had his hands tied up, restrained so he couldn't pull out all those tubes and plugs. He asked me, "Won't you loosen my hands?" and that just kills you . . . you can't do it. I could hardly stand it then so I thought maybe I do need some coffee. Anyhow, I went. And when I came back he was gone.

Mrs. Callahan has tried to get along alone as best she can. She wonders whether she should go out and get a job. She wonders whether she should move. She's lonely, but she feels at home at the lake. She's afraid that she might be unhappy if she were in another place. She is afraid that she might make a move that wouldn't work out, and then she'd be worse off than she is now.

She continues to try to get guidance from her husband. In a way, she is still relying on him to help her make decisions. When she has a question, she tries to figure out what he would say under the circumstances.

Mrs. Callahan believes Mr. Callahan is there with her. She feels that if she moves from the house, which Mr. Callahan loved very much, she will be disloyal to him. If she doesn't go to the cemetery, he will know that she hasn't come and will think, she fears, that she's beginning to forget him. She's afraid to get a job because she thinks she might be too old. If she were working, she would have to leave the house unattended for long periods of time. If she leaves the house unattended, she somehow feels, she's leaving her husband unattended too—something she never did.

These are the dilemmas that face Mrs. Callahan daily. They keep her frozen into a place where she can't make a decision. She is far from resolving her grief and moving on with her life. She seems too locked-in by guilt to feel that she has a right to a life of her own, now that no one depends on her.

Mrs. Callahan summed up her most poignant fear:

> Well, one thing that does worry you is you do think, I'm getting older now, and what will happen. I'd hate to get sick and lay in a rest home. I don't have that many people to take care of me and I wouldn't want them to have a burden like that anyway, but, that is the biggest worry I have . . . of just getting older, wondering what is going to happen to me.

There was a difference in the Tampa Study between how older spouses reacted as opposed to younger ones. I found that younger spouses initially showed greater shock, confusion, and personal death anxiety, as well as guilt. At follow-up two years later, however, younger spouses had begun to face life once again. They seemed motivated by hope, which helped them to resolve their dilemmas more easily.

Older spouses, rather than moving on toward a new life, had instead a heightening of their grief reaction. Despite their courage and faith, it became increasingly difficult to hold on to their optimistic outlook for the future. Not only was time running out and their physical health becoming more tenuous, but, worst of all, being alone meant deprivation of any companionship or love.

Turning Grief Around—Steps in Renewal

It took time for Mrs. Callahan to deal with the many decisions concerning her life. Hard choices faced her, but taking things one step at a time proved to be the proper avenue for her (as it is for most of us). In the beginning, she didn't have the insight to know what was a step forward, what was simply a holding pattern, or what was a regression in her progress. She "played it as it came," she said.

The Decision to Live Again

Probably her hardest decision was determining whether she had the will to begin again. At age sixty-two, she was afraid it might be too late. Yet, from somewhere within herself, she was able to pull out some strength to make a small start. As she put it:

> I don't know whether it's time or what. They always talk about time . . . but I don't know . . . no particular thing . . . just gradually. I felt so bad for so long . . . then I think in the last few months I started to feel a little better . . . maybe I just made up my mind that I've got to do something. Pull myself out some way. There's only really one person can do it, that's yourself . . . I guess.

Making a Start—Contacting Children and Friends

She began to call a few of her friends and arrange to have lunch. Getting out seemed to add some new energy. She talked to her two daughters every week, and although they lived in California, they began offering some suggestions for her life in Florida. For the first time since Mr. Callahan had died, she began to open herself to some new possibilities.

Attending a Support Group

One important step for her was attending a Widow-to-Widow group and hearing the stories of other women.

Seeing the progress of others gave her some hope that she might actually get through her sad experience. While she was there, she learned about a retired tax consultant who had helped several women deal with their smaller incomes, at no charge. After working with him, she was able to figure out a budget that made her feel a little safer. He gave her some good suggestions on selling her house and reinvesting the income.

Registering for a Course

Through the Widow-to-Widow group, she learned about a course offered at the local junior college on how to live as a single person. The course gave information on shopping, cooking, entertaining, investing, and traveling, and there was no exam! She enrolled for the next session.

Making New Friends and Preparing to Move

The first night at the singles course, Mrs. Callahan met a woman about her own age, who eventually became her best friend. Her new friend introduced her to others, and her friendship circle increased. These were new people who hadn't known her in her old life, so her new start was really beginning. Her new friend showed her two or three very attractive houses that were for sale in her development. It didn't seem so frightening to move to an area where she knew people.

Releasing Her Husband

Mrs. Callahan's hardest task was letting go of her husband so that she could let go of the lake house. The two were so closely tied together. This took longer than she thought it would, and she was insistent that she had to be thoroughly

ready when she did it. Finally, Mrs. Callahan found the
peace she had sought and was able to reconcile herself to her
husband's death and release him. She told me at our last
meeting together:

> I feel that after this long a time, it's been closer to three
> years, that I made up my mind that I've had to realize that
> he's gone, he's probably happy and that everything should be
> all right. I'd love to have him back, but I'd hate to see him
> suffer the way he did the last year. So . . . you have to think
> of those things, too. 'Cause he did suffer so much at the last.
> He didn't enjoy things like he used to and he didn't . . .
> couldn't hardly eat anymore. When you get to the place
> where you don't enjoy food and have to take a bunch of
> pills . . . and you don't want to take pills . . . he just
> wasn't getting much out of life anymore. That does make it
> hard.

COMFORTS IN BEREAVEMENT

Support Systems

We desperately need the help of friends in getting through
bereavement. We human beings are herd animals and we
need the support of people who love us and accept our ups
and down. In the Tampa Study, when asked what was the
greatest help in getting through their loss, people overwhelmingly said, "Friends and family." There are no substitutes. George Mackenzie proudly told me that eighty-four
friends had come to his house between his wife's death and
the funeral. They had brought him the help that held him
together during those awful days. I remember what a comfort it was for friends to call, to drop by, to bring me
anything—food, flowers, whatever. Those gifts made me
feel more special and loved, and I was grateful for each
remembrance.

Sensing the Mate's Presence

The habits of a long marriage are not easily forgotten. Having a partner in the home, talking, eating, sleeping together—all are taken for granted over the years. Our perceptions of these interactions don't stop just because one of the partners is gone. We often sense the presence of the lost spouse and usually are comforted by these experiences. Several of the bereaved spouses in the Tampa Study told me of actually seeing their mates in their homes after the funeral. Mrs. Martin said:

> It was kind of strange. I was standing at the sink doing dishes like always and I was thinking about Herb . . . how he used to come in after supper and stand around and talk. This night, I thought I heard him call my name from down the hall, but when I looked he was gone. I actually answered him before I realized what I was doing. . . . still, I had the strangest feeling like he was really there . . . like he was really calling my name.

After my mother died, I often had the feeling that she was near me. I had what I call the "flicker phenomenon": I would perceive a shadow in the peripheral vision of my eye. I would immediately think of Mother and quickly look up, fully expecting to see her. I never did, but I don't doubt that her energy was there in some form or another.

For most of us who have had a similar experience, there is comfort in the thought that our loved ones are nearby and may be trying to let us know that they are safe and unharmed. We feel watched over and guided, which is gratifying when we are in a time of such chaos and confusion.

Remarriage

When we have recently lost our mate, remarriage is the last thing on our minds. We are too filled with the deprivations, the longings to have him or her back, the searing separation anxiety that keeps us afraid and insecure. As time somehow moves us inextricably toward healing, we become more aware of our need to assuage our loneliness. Some manage this by developing friends to go out with, but they block out any thought of a permanent relationship. Mr. Thalinger lost his wife of twenty-six years and didn't want to tie himself down again:

> I don't think I'll ever remarry . . . I don't think so. I enjoy taking ladies out to dinner and stuff like that . . . as far as marriage is concerned, I don't think I want to get married. A lot of people think that . . . but right now I don't think I would. I enjoy the company of ladies, but as far as getting into a permanent marriage situation, it's not my plan.

From research that has been done, it looks as if two years is not enough time to let go of one relationship and start another. Yet, several people who needed a replacement started over as soon as they could find someone. Mr. Brown knew from the beginning that he didn't like to live alone, didn't want to, and had no intention of trying it. He found a suitable companion and was married within six months after his wife died. Unfortunately, he hadn't given grief enough time and had expectations from the new marriage that couldn't be fulfilled. Because he had been in a happy marriage before, he thought that he could make it continue. When he separated, he gave himself time to heal before thinking of remarriage again.

In another situation, Bob, a widower, married a woman whom he had known for years and who was in his social circle. She had six children, four of whom were still living at home. However, this didn't seem to be an obstacle to Bob. He bought a larger house and incorporated the whole family. The marriage was successful. It had been a happy decision for them both.

Remarriage can bring much comfort, but, if the expectations are too high, only disappointment will emerge. I strongly suggest waiting until a new identity has been found. Grief changes us. There is no way we will ever be the same person, after a significant loss. We need time to slip out of one shell before growing another. Our values change. If we continue to grow, what we want out of life will broaden to include many new facets. Time is needed. When we are ready, grief will be behind us and a new life will open up to us.

9

On Becoming an Adult Orphan— A Parent Dies

> Every daughter looks forward to the time when she can
> become friends with her mother, you know, past the time
> when the mother–daughter role is maintained. Usually
> this comes when the daughter has children of her own and
> can fully realize what the mother has experienced. . . .
> Well, my sisters had both reached this point, and I never
> did. I think now of the friend I missed having.
>
> *Twenty-five-year-old daughter,*
> *following the death of her mother*

We have always thought of
orphans as small waifs forlornly lost in some large and impersonal institution. Some orphans fulfill that image, but
generally it is an exaggerated stereotype of an old-fashioned
notion. We can be orphaned in many different ways; we
don't have to be small or young. There are lots of orphaned
grown-ups around.

Whether we have lost one or both of our parents, we still
feel like an orphan. The longer we have our parents with us,
the more comfortable we feel, as if we will have them here
forever, and the greater our shock when we are suddenly in
the world without them.

Most of us will lose our parents when we are in our fifties
or sixties. The remarkable successes of medical science and

positive health conditioning have contributed to the extension of life for older people by controlling many killer diseases. Ours has become a four- or five-generation society. Such longevity suggests eternal life on earth, supporting a false notion that we will be here forever, along with our parents and children.

OUR PARENTS: OUR BUFFERS

As we approach middle age, we become aware that our parents are growing older. Mother or Dad might stumble slightly, or rest more, or move more slowly. I remember when my brother had been away on a long trip and visited Mother before he went on home to Miami. I was at Mother's for dinner and when she was out of the room, Jimmy turned to me with a worried look and said, "Mother has gotten so old while I was away. What happened?" Mother hadn't changed much to me, but during the year he had been away she had gotten older in his eyes. "She's started to show deeper lines in her face," he said. I was shocked to hear him say this and became rather defensive, retorting, "Of course she hasn't aged. She looks great." But his observation made me stop and think.

We are usually given some preparation for the death of a parent just by realizing that it is the inevitable and natural order of things. We *expect* to outlive our parents. However, more issues are involved than we may realize. By recognizing that our parents are growing older, we begin to see that we are growing older too. With the realization that they could die, we see the buffer against our own death removed. As long as our parents live, we will also be around. Take them away, and we're next.

Grief and fear are our natural responses. We experience anticipatory grief for our parents' inevitable death, and fear of our own aging and death. These emotions contribute to our feeling of loss as we get older, and are probably factors in the infamous "midlife crisis." When we reach middle age, losses of one kind or another seem endless. When our parent dies, the death usually propels us into a more responsible position within the family. Our parent is no longer there to fall back on, and we have been moved into first position—we are next in line. The death of our parent during our adulthood can be regarded as part of the natural order of human dynamics, but most of us, especially if our parent is still active, are emotionally unprepared to let our parent go.

Judy was thirty-five when her mother died. She was the youngest in a family of three daughters, and was probably the closest to her mother. Her mother used to say that she and Judy were very much alike in their sentimental ways—more open to showing feelings, more easily hurt. Judy would always go to her mother with problems. She knew that she would receive a sympathetic listening and good advice.

Judy was an excellent music teacher and had a large number of students whom she taught in her home. She had been married for ten years but had no children. She told me that she had always planned to have some but had been too busy. Besides, she still felt like her mother's little girl, she said, not ready for the responsibility of motherhood.

When her mother became ill with cancer, Judy was more frightened than at any other time in her life. By the time the tumor was discovered, the disease had metastasized throughout her mother's body. The illness was swift and deadly. Judy's mother died in her arms, with the rest of the family around her bedside. Her death was impossible for Judy to comprehend and she remained in shock for several months.

Recovery was slow for Judy. She had several serious setbacks during her bereavement, which further complicated her already unsteady progress. First, her marriage disintegrated and she was divorced. She lived alone now. Heavy financial difficulties followed, which naturally resulted in much worry. When her twelve-year-old cat was hit by a car and killed, Judy felt completely lost and abandoned. When I saw her two years after her mother's death, she told me:

> When Mother was gone, I knew that I had to grow up—
> start accepting responsibility without leaning on her. Many
> of the times I didn't actually go to her for help but I knew
> she was there if I needed her. All that is changed now. I
> must see things through myself.

When I asked Judy whether she felt her mother's presence, she said that she did in a general way—not specifically
sensing her being in the room, but feeling her mother's aura.
When I asked her whether she felt her mother guiding her,
she began to cry and nodded "Yes." Judy had been quite
stoic up to that point, but thinking about her mother in
such a poignant manner made her miss her all the more.

The parental role doesn't disappear with a parent's death.
As adult children, we still feel the guidance we have grown
used to. We tend to carry an ideal memory of our parents as
loving people who guided us through the stormy times and
the good periods of our lives.

For some of us, the memories may not be ideal. We may
remember a controlling parent, an alcoholic parent, or a parent who expected perfection from us. We still hear a critical
voice echoing in our lives; when our parents die, we are left
to somehow work through the painful ambivalence. Our
bereavement will be longer because we not only have to deal
with the love–hate aspects of our relationship and be willing
to take our own power back from them, but we must let go
of our guilt and shame responses to the critical voice.

The Parent–Child Bond

The parent–child bond represents the longest tie of our life.
It is established in infancy and creates an attachment that
endures well into old age. Our parents are a part of us. Beyond the strong genetic connection based on our physical
and mental qualities, our most important parental bond develops through our social connection—characteristics we
learned from our parents during our developmental years.

Whether our relationships with our parents were negative, ambivalent, or very positive, we are deeply influenced by our parents' presence.

Our parents helped us form our images and our sense of ourselves. They supplied the early input to our self-concept. Many of the feelings that we have as adults have been influenced by the way in which our parents responded to us as children. It is amazing how our parents can make us feel like happy children again by a simple word or action or, at another time, with just a look or gesture, cause us to feel guilt and shame that we thought were long gone. Their effect on us takes us by surprise. When they die, we are just as surprised that we feel abandoned and vulnerable, like children again.

Our Age When a Parent Dies

The younger we are, the stronger is our attachment to our parents. Our childhood memories of dependency and neediness are fresher in our minds when we are children and adolescents than when we are mature adults. When we are little, we look to our parents to "fix" things for us. They help solve our problems, provide for us, and nurture and comfort us. As we grow toward young adulthood and become more self-sufficient and independent, we begin to take on some of these responsibilities for ourselves. The loss of a parent when we are young leaves us, like Judy, with the realization that we must now fend for ourselves. The parent who was our strong support is gone.

Ages Twenty to Thirty-Five

During these years, we usually experience the broad transition of moving from our family of origin to our family of marriage. Our careers take a great deal of energy and concern as we struggle to build our feelings of independence and self-reliance. Although we may still rely on our parents for approval, we are gradually moving into friendship patterns with them rather than maintaining the parent–child relationship. Raising our own children helps us to identify with our parents more strongly because we begin to see the problems they faced. The death of a parent at this time means the loss of an important role model as well as a close friend and ally.

Ages Thirty-Five to Fifty-Five

These middle years are still taken up with career, family, and personal concerns. Our developmental shift toward midlife creates new feelings about our own aging, especially as we see our parents growing older. Our parents may require more of our time or may need appropriate care. The death of a parent during these years begins to foreshadow our own demise. We are face-to-face with the realizations that we will certainly die too and that we are moving well past the halfway mark of life.

Age Fifty-Five On

From age fifty-five on, we face the possibility of having to place our parent in a chronic care facility. A role reversal begins to take place: we may see our parents becoming like dependent children. There is often a problem of psychological and social death because of Alzheimer's disease, stroke, or senility. We may watch a parent, previously energetic and vital, sink slowly into a weakened and debilitated state. Death, during this time, can be a blessed release from suffering. Yet, our own tragic loss of a love object, like losing a dependent child, is heartbreaking.

WHAT WE LOSE WHEN A PARENT DIES

Special Love

Few loves are as unconditional as that of a beloved parent. In a good relationship, a parent has supported and guided us through the somewhat rocky journey of growing up.

Mother and Dad got mad when we disappointed them, but somehow we always knew they loved us just the same. Maggie, fifty-five, who lost her mother suddenly, following a lethal stroke, wrote:

> Someone of greatest importance had suddenly gone from me. I was completely bereft, stunned as I never anticipated it. The only one who ever truly loved me was gone from this world. The world felt empty, and I lonely.

When we lose this love, we feel deprived. We somehow know that we will never again have a love like this.

Being Someone's Child

It's wonderful how, as adults, we revert back to feeling like a kid every now and then. It feels good to have moments when responsibility doesn't weigh heavily on us and we don't feel so grown-up. Having a parent tell amusing anecdotes about us as children can bring on this feeling. When this happens, we are still children at heart and can relive, through our parent's memories, what it feels like to be a kid again. When we lose a parent, we lose our childhood. There is no one else who shared that part of our lives as our parent did.

A Dear Friend

As we grow older, our relationship with a parent gradually shifts from parent–child to one of reciprocal friendship. As the power struggle naturally minimizes, there are fewer reasons to argue or become displeased with each other. We develop an easier manner and are more relaxed when we are together. When we lose our parent, we lose an irreplaceable friendship, one that has developed and grown over a long period of time.

If our relationship with our parent has never quite reached true reciprocity and we are still hoping to achieve that new and easier level, the death of our parent robs us of that opportunity. If there are things in the past that we feel we need to make right with a parent, the death cuts short that opportunity and we miss the chance.

My daughter, Catherine, pregnant five and a half months, had lost her baby during a traumatic stillbirth. This happened only two months before her father's death. She mourned the two events as one; she couldn't separate them. Catherine wrote in her journal shortly after her father died:

My father was growing weaker daily and breathing was a huge struggle. My two sisters came from Tenn. and Cal. and my mother from N.C. and we tried to help him. Actually, by the time the family arrived he was back in the hospital (after two weeks trying to make it at home) and within a week, he chose to discontinue all medicine and take morphine and Valium injections hourly. Three days before that we were all with him; in fact, we were taking shifts so he wouldn't be alone. I had the all-nighter before he died and watched him slipping, his breathing becoming more and more bubbly, every slightest action taxing him terribly. He could hardly speak. The next morning an hour after I left, he gave up.

He had been a golden gloves boxer, an aviator, a thinker, and a provocateur. And he was truly a fighter, so I can only imagine that he calculated his odds and knew the next step would be a respirator. He would have none of that, nor radiation or chemotherapy. He died a long sleep, in the midst of four women who loved him deeply, who tried to ease him through that door to whatever flight awaited him. We prayed endlessly and remembered songs he'd sung to us in childhood, and we sang them softly to him. And we cried on and on and on.

He died two months to the day after the baby died, and I can't help feeling that my life has been lopped off at the beginning and the end, prelife and postlife, the seed that sprung me and the seed I sprung. I'm trying to make sense of these deaths, a son and a father, and the only thing I can make out is a sad thing: I was so wrapped up grieving for a little unborn creature that I failed to notice the tower toppling. He was growing so sick and I wasn't paying attention as I should have been. It became apparent to me then, when he was really sick, that my prayers for him to live were selfish ones, so I might have a second opportunity to take care of him, since I had failed the first. The two nights I sat up with him before he died were all he could give me—such a little time to expiate such great guilt.

I know we all will have our death, and it's all we can hope, I suppose, that we can choose the time, the morphine, and to be surrounded by those who love us. That's lucky, I guess.

It was a long time before Catherine could reconcile both her losses. She agonized over the feeling that she didn't do enough for her father when he was sick. Because he had always been able to "fix" things for her when she was little, unconsciously she wanted to do the same for him now. Somehow, she needed and wanted to keep him from dying. When he died, she felt that she had lost the opportunity to show him that she truly loved him.

A Grandparent for our Children

There's a lot to be said about the pride we feel when our parents brag about their grandchildren. For us, the parents, a deep sense of satisfaction comes from seeing all three generations connecting. The wonderful continuity of life makes us feel safe. Grandparents add a dimension to our children's lives. They are often a source of wisdom, kindness, and patience. When we lose our parents, we lose not only the connection and the safety, but also the sense of accomplishment that they convey. They are proud of us because we have produced such wonderful grandchildren and we have kept the lineage intact. Their immortality is secured through this lineage.

WHEN WE LOSE BOTH
PARENTS WITHIN A SHORT TIME

Losing both parents is a terrible possibility, but it does happen. Medical science has shown that, because grief lowers the immune system's resistance, the death of a spouse can lead to illness and even death of the other spouse. When this happens, the surviving adult children hardly have time to process one death before the other one occurs. The "double" death can lead to prolonged grief and intense feelings of being twice "orphaned."

Julie was twenty-eight when her mother died. Being the youngest of four children, she told me, she was probably spoiled by her mother, to whom she was very close. She said she never took advantage of the good things her mother offered to her and always tried to reciprocate in some way. When her mother contracted cancer, there was a valiant fight to save her, but she succumbed eventually to the disease.

Julie described her mother's death as the worst thing that had ever happened to her. The fact that this was her first death experience contributed to the horror of the situation. She grieved constantly for over six months, crying every day. Her work went downhill, she said, and she was thankful that her boss was understanding. "He was probably the only one who did understand. Every one else wanted me back the way I was."

Julie's parents had been happily married for forty-five years. She told me that they had been devoted to each other and were wonderful role models. Naturally, when her mother got sick, her father was by her side almost every minute. To her father, her mother's death represented both a terrible loss and a tragic defeat. Julie said, "Dad took care of everyone else during the funeral. We were amazed at how well he held up. I guess I leaned on him too much. I just couldn't get by my own grief to think much about him."

Shortly after the death, Julie and her husband were transferred to Florida. She didn't feel that she was deserting her father, because three other sisters lived near him. Soon after the move, her sisters wrote that their father was spending more and more time closed up in the house. He seemed to have lost all desire to see anyone. They assumed it was the natural course of grief, and thought that he would come through it in due time.

Julie's father didn't come through it. The neighbors said that he spent his evenings just sitting in the dark. They grew worried about him and began buying sweet rolls for him and putting them on his porch early every morning. He always took them in, and the neighbors felt reassured that they had at least made some contact.

One morning, the rolls stayed there all day. His next-door neighbor broke into the house and found him dead. He had, apparently, suffered a heart attack. Curled up on his bed, he was holding his wife's picture close to his chest. Without her, his will to live was gone.

Needless to say, Julie struggled with terrible guilt: if she had not gone to Florida, she said, she might have been able to help him. Then, remembering her own grief, she wondered whether she had had the energy to do any more than help herself. We all have similar thoughts. Could we have done a little more? If we had given our parent a little extra time, might he or she still be alive now?

Fortunately, these guilt feelings will usually work themselves out in time, particularly if we can share our thoughts with a trusted friend or counselor. Nothing is ever as bad, once we have used our courage to openly express our feelings.

WHEN OUR PARENT DIES FROM CHRONIC ILLNESS

Just as our guilt concerning something we did or didn't do causes us much pain in bereavement, so does the memory of watching our parent suffer a slow and deteriorating illness. When we've always seen our parents as strong and capable, watching them grow physically weaker, particularly when they are in excessive pain, can be one of the hardest experiences we'll ever have to endure. For this type of loss, the grief before the death is often much worse than the grief after the death.

Whenever there is a debilitating illness leading to eventual death, we see a social death that takes place long before the physical one. When a parent, who all through life has been socially active, is forced to give up connections with friends and activities, it is a dying that matches the pain of the slow physical death. As one forty-three-year-old daughter said:

Mom was the liveliest person around. . . . she was great. Until she got sick, she could match energy with the best of them. . . . loved to dance. I remember last spring at my daughter's wedding, she had Dad out on the dance floor half the night. He was exhausted but she was still raring to go.

Then in August, they found the tumor in her stomach. I couldn't believe how fast she went down after the chemotherapy. She was so sick . . . lost so much weight. She was just skin and bones at the last. . . . God, I hate the disease for doing that to her . . . it just wasn't fair.

When our childhood memories are of a beautiful and vigorous mother who is capable of taking on almost anything, watching her become dependent, impaired, and helpless can be the worst grief of all. We see it happen in other families but never dream it's going to happen in ours. This is a steady, painful, slow death for everyone involved.

Once the death has occurred, however, there is often a sense of relief that our parent doesn't have to suffer any longer. The pain is now ended, even if the hurt is still there for us. Some expectancy of death, no matter how difficult, usually leads to less intense grief after the death. The shock is not as severe or prolonged as when a death is sudden. We are able to move through the phases of grief more rapidly.

WHEN WE MUST
INSTITUTIONALIZE OUR PARENT

There is often extreme grief when we find that we must place a parent in a nursing home. It is everyone's wish that a parent should be as comfortable and happy as possible all through life, but especially during old age, when self-care is more difficult. However, a nursing home is sometimes the only alternative. I am not saying that all nursing homes represent bad situations. I just know, from past experience, that no one makes impersonal care in impersonal surroundings a first choice. We'd all rather stay in our own comfortable environment as long as possible.

When a chronic care facility is the only way to go, we, as adult children, often feel like executioners. Because of this move, our parent will lose the way of life that was valued and familiar. This is a social death, and we feel deeply guilty that a treasured life should end this way.

When our parent is mentally impaired from Alzheimer's disease, stroke, or senility and there is need for constant care, a nursing home is usually the only alternative. Initially, we may feel relieved that care is available and that we are managing to get some well-deserved rest for ourselves. As time goes by, however, the sadness and sorrow mount. The horror of watching our parent deteriorate is sometimes more than we can bear. I've heard of many sad cases of adult children who stopped visiting altogether because either they thought their parent didn't know who they were there, or they just didn't have the stomach to go there any longer.

OUR NEED FOR
SUPPORT IN BEREAVEMENT

When I was a postdoctoral fellow at Cushing Hospital, a geriatric hospital in Framingham, Massachusetts, I worked with many families who had institutionalized their parents there. One adult daughter visited twice each day to feed, bathe, and change her mother. Her mother, an Alzheimer's patient, was like a dependent child and became a focus of concern for her. One would have thought that, with the inevitability of the situation, death would be a relief for both of them, but the daughter mourned intensely after her mother died. Months went by, and the grief seemed as severe as it had been in the beginning. Her husband and married son were helpless to know what to do. It was as if she had lost a child. Emotionally, she had. Yet, because her mother was old, impaired, and debilitated, she found no social support among her friends. They were, instead, eager to have her back the way she was before her mother became sick. When they saw that she couldn't shake her grief, they began to leave her alone, suggesting she get professional help because they couldn't fix things for her. Fortunately, she was able to find a supportive counselor who normalized her grief by helping her to see that her loss was great and that grief can't be hurried.

The death of a parent represents a significant loss, in many respects. Yet, when the funeral is over, our society expects us to pick up exactly as things were before. People rarely inquire into our personal feelings or even acknowledge our grief, after a week or two. There appears to be impatience with the grief of a bereaved adult child, as though it does not require much attention or long-term reaction. After my mother died, friends who didn't know her would ask how old she was. When I said eighty-one, they would nod and comment on what a long life she had lived, as if she were ready to die. It made me furious. Mother wasn't nearly ready to die. She was alive, vigorous, and youthful. The truth was, I wasn't ready to have her die. I needed time and I wanted permission to grieve as long as I needed. That permission was rarely offered.

How can another person say what event will trigger the deepest grief in our lives? Much depends on the type and quality of each relationship, the strength of the attachment we share with others. It seems natural to shift dependency needs from parents to spouse—and, perhaps, to children—

when moving into and through adulthood. As our husbands and children begin to require time and attention, we gradually disengage from the activities that we previously shared with a parent. Even so, a parent represents strong attachments, and we find a certain number of ongoing needs are still reciprocal at any age. When we realize the many ties we have with a parent, his or her death is met with feelings of enormous deprivation and, consequently, a sense of deep personal loss.

10

How the Family Grieves

I remember how rotten my family acted. They came up here and made a big scene at the hospital the day he died, instead of giving me comfort. . . . I get so angry even now. I go to bed and all these things start spinning through my head . . . and that has never happened before. After the depression lifted, . . . all this anger was going through my head at these people, who incidentally, I've never seen again . . . . So I made some decisions what to do about them. I wouldn't put myself in that position again, to be treated that way. So, in other words, I don't want to ever see them again.

Widow, age 49

When we consider bereavement, we usually think in terms of separate individuals—a grieving spouse, a bereaved parent, or an orphaned child. Research has led us to focus on individual grief because most studies have examined the symptoms of individuals rather than the family unit as a whole. But make no mistake: grief is a family affair. When we lose a member, the entire family is affected. It is like losing an important link in a chain. Before the chain can be effective again, we have to repair, rejoin, or replace the missing link. The process is often disruptive and painful until a balance can be reestablished, whether that balance is healthy or not.

FAMILY BALANCING

The balance of a family doesn't have to be healthy to maintain itself. Some families are terribly dysfunctional but maintain a status quo. An alcoholic father may be balanced by an enabling wife, and the children may act out in order to take attention from the alcoholic father. The status quo is kept until something interferes to change the chain of command. Suppose the wife dies. The one who balanced the entire family is now gone, and two sides are acting out with no one to mediate. Either the father must sober up, relieving the kids of their need to distract attention from him, or one of the children must take the mother's place and become the enabler and balancer. Until something creates a balance again, there is chaos as the family attempts to find an equilibrium.

FACTORS CREATING PROBLEMS IN GRIEF

Four factors seem to cause the greatest disruption in family functioning after a death:

1. The timing of the death in the life cycle. Did a child or an elderly member die? The most disruptive situations come when an individual dies in the prime of life, when others are dependent on him or her.
2. The nature of the death—sudden versus anticipated. Death that is sudden produces the greatest shock to the individuals and the family system. There is no time to soothe ambivalences, to say good-bye, to adjust to a new way of functioning.
3. The closed family system. Feelings of privacy and lack of communication within the family mark this type of system. Outsiders are considered intruders and, within the family, a conspiracy of silence is maintained.
4. The position held in the family by the deceased member. The more emotionally significant a family

member is in a family, the greater the emotional impact when that member dies.

A family will need to reestablish a different hierarchy after a death. There is, however, an opportunity for the family to grow together and become more cohesive by trying to sort out and share the feelings and emotions with which they must deal.

Family Members' Grief

Families often face a difficult challenge because every member's grief is different from the others'. People simply don't grieve alike. Our personalities vary even within a small nuclear family. One person might be generally quiet and hold feelings in; another might be more demonstrative and show feelings more readily. Some members may have greater frustration tolerance than others.

Moreover, family roles are different. The oldest sibling is probably the most responsible, possibly relating to the parents in a nearly adult way. The youngest sibling is more likely to look to friends for social support than to the parents. Within the family, members relate to each other differently. When one dies, each member's loss is a little different from the others'. Because the relationships vary, the grief varies as well.

Anger

The stress of bereavement creates a high level of tension and irritability. This, in turn, often causes bereaved persons to react in anger and hostility toward situations and family members whom, under normal circumstances, they would probably ignore. We often take our anger out on those closest to us. If we don't usually show our anger, this display can be most distressing. It doesn't feel right—it's not like us at all. We feel different and out of control.

Anger can be expressed in many ways. Some of us explode and verbalize our anger. Others act out, abusing alcohol or defying authority. Still others turn anger inward and withdraw, which is probably the most lethal expression of anger because it is transformed into repressed shame and guilt. When it is deeply inside ourselves, anger ferments and festers, continuing to torment us with unhappiness and desperation. I have seen family members who maintained an angry distance from a sister, brother, or other relative for years, after a misunderstanding originating after a death. Freeing ourselves from this poison can take months or years. If it is not dealt with, however, it can erupt into physical symptoms and illnesses later on.

OPEN AND CLOSED FAMILIES

Open Families

The more that families can communicate thoughts and feelings before a loss, the better a family will deal with grief when it happens. Remaining open is perhaps one of the most important things a family can learn, in order to guard against misunderstandings that often arise at the time of a death. If we know someone is dealing honestly with us and has no hidden emotional agenda, then we know where we stand with that person. We feel safer with him or her than with someone who hides feelings. Honesty is the essential basis for intimacy.

Closed Families

When family members do not share their feelings with each other or maintain a conspiracy of silence with outsiders, they are living in closed families. As children, they were taught not to feel, not to talk, and not to trust. Adult children of alcoholics are a prime example. They were, most often, brought up in a family where conflict was never discussed and where abuse, either physical or emotional, was present but never alluded to. Many of these children grow up to have closed families of their own.

These families may be quite successful socially, with many superficial friends; to all the world, they look confident and charming. On the inside, however, they are usually afraid the acting won't be done perfectly—that their own performances won't be perfect, and that, if they are not careful, others will be able to detect the flaws.

This is stagnant, for many reasons. The two reasons that relate to bereavement are:

1. People who remain stoic and silent will receive no emotional support from others. Bereavement is a time when friends are a necessity. In the Tampa Study, when I asked bereaved people what helped them most in getting through their grief, they almost always answered, "Friends and family." We need friends who will stay with us whether we are weeping in despair or screaming at the top of our lungs in fury. We need friends to whom we won't be afraid to expose ourselves at those vulnerable moments.

2. Unless the family begins to change, the conspiracy of silence will be perpetuated and family members will be stuck in that mode forever. So often, if only one member changes in attitude, the others will change too. One person's different reaction can automatically force others to change their typical way of responding.

CHILDREN'S BEREAVEMENT

Even young children can comprehend death, if clear and realistic information is provided. They can deal with death, especially when loving support helps them to understand the facts and feelings involved. However, as a rule, children are notoriously excluded from death in American families.

We try to keep death a secret, sometimes even from the dying person. We are a death-denying culture that tries to "protect" children from the "morbid truth." In doing this, we tend to alienate children from life, because death is a very important part of life. We block their emotional growth, leaving them ill-prepared to deal with future losses, which will inevitably arise.

I described earlier how I was "shipped off" to close friends' house after my aunt's death at our home. I didn't know these friends of Mother very well and, being shy, I had a hard time with strangers. I cried myself to sleep that first night, harboring horrible fears that Mother would die too and no one would ever come to get me.

When Mother did come for me, I didn't dare mention my aunt, for fear she would somehow come back to scare me or punish me for something. When children are left to their own thoughts without real information, they can dream up the worst possible fears.

Some children are given more details than they are equipped to process. Too much description can readily confuse a small child, so it is best to allow children to ask the questions they need to have answered. If no questions are forthcoming, a lead-in can be supplied: "We loved Uncle Joe, didn't we? We're really going to miss him." The child, knowing that talk of Uncle Joe is open, will be encouraged to ask more questions.

Children need to grieve at their own pace, but their fears need to be dealt with directly. Depending on the age of the child, death can be terrifying. It is hard for anyone to accept the finality of death; for a child, it is sometimes impossible. Children will try to fantasize the return of the deceased. Small children may ask only a few questions concerning a recent death, and then race outside to join their playmates, seeming to forget the conversation. We have to remember that children process information differently from adults. Adults must be patient with their questions, answering only those questions that the children need answered.

When parents can be sensitive to their child's grief and need to mourn, they can help the child to share the longing in his or her heart. A child needs the opportunity to talk with others about yearnings, feelings, and precious memories.

SIBLINGS' BEREAVEMENT

A grief that gets very little attention is that caused by loss of a brother or sister in childhood and adolescence. In my experience, when a child dies, the remaining siblings have a hard time in discharging their grief, for two reasons: the parents are caught up in their own impossible pain and haven't the ability to focus beyond it, and the normal ambivalence or "survivor guilt" experienced by the remaining siblings is translated into deep-seated guilt and shame.

Ambivalence is present in all sibling relationships. We can all remember how angry we could get at a brother or sister from time to time. At the very height of fury, we might have said "Get lost" or "Drop dead." We certainly didn't expect them to die, but what if it had happened? What if a sibling had died right after we had said something like that? We can only imagine the horrible guilt and shame we would have borne. Our meanness would have been too awful to even tell anyone about, especially during adolescence, when feelings were so hard to talk about anyhow.

Survivor guilt comes not only from feeling guilty that we are alive and the other person is dead, but also from the feeling that we were somehow responsible for the death, unrealistic as that may seem.

Survivor guilt afflicts every member of a family. The mother may feel extreme guilt for not protecting the dead child from this terrible tragedy. The father may feel anger at the forces that robbed him of his child and, because he can't change anything, he may feel powerless and out of control. The remaining siblings may feel their own guilt for having survived, especially because there is a tendency to idealize a dead brother or sister. Too often, the child who died is seen as the brightest, the most attractive, or the most talented or athletic. If the parents perpetuate this fantasy, the surviving children will grow up in the shadow of the dead sibling, trying to fill in for him or her and never realizing an identity of their own.

Implicit in children's survivor guilt is the fear of not being able to measure up to the parents' expectation, now that the survivors must carry more of the burden of responsibility.

I heartily recommend that parents include the siblings in discussions about the dead child. Adolescents, particularly, need to share in some of the plans surrounding the rituals. In that way, they can feel identified as part of the family and will be more open to sharing their thoughts and feelings. For younger siblings, I feel it is important for parents and family members to use touch as often as possible. All children need the "safety net" of love and affection to reassure them that they still have a treasured place in the family. Equally important, they need to know that their parents will not die immediately too or that death won't happen to them now. In the shelter of a close and loving family, children of all ages will be able to accept death without lasting negative consequences.

With the reduction of family size, it becomes imperative to think of extending our "family" to include nonbiologic kin. Sometimes we can do this through bereavement support groups such as Compassionate Friends, or Widow-to-Widow. Churches used to be centers for social connections as well as spiritual enhancement, and some still are. However, for the most part, families have become desocialized in churches, attending services but not participating in the secular activities. Twelve-step groups probably come the closest to forming a "family" with lasting friendships. Because these groups are based on honesty and open sharing, the people who join them feel at home together.

We all long for an ideal family, but most of us don't come close. We'll probably never achieve the ideal, but I think we give up too easily on having a close relationship.

11

The Power of Mourning Rituals

When that freight car came up on the tracks and the doors opened, there stood the guard beside my father's casket. A guard went with the undertaker and we went home. Later, when the undertaker brought Dad back to the house, I went upstairs until the undertaker was gone . . . and when I came down, in the front parlor behind the screen, they had put a beige, dark beige velvet, three screens really and they had taken my father's last big portrait, and hung that at the head and the citations at the foot.

All the funerals were held right there in the home. In fact, you didn't go to the church very often. Funeral homes weren't popular in my hometown. Everybody came to the family . . . big baskets of food, family next to the casket . . . distant relatives back in the kitchen and neighbors upstairs. How much more comforting . . . .

Adult child, age 22

The rituals at death provide the glue that holds us together during those awful first days of grief. We generally move through them in a daze, not really aware of what is going on around us. It is as if we are being led blindfolded from one place to another by other people who can see. The early rituals—the wake, the funeral or memorial service, the burial—move us relentlessly from place to place, providing direction at a time when we feel terribly lost.

Different losses produce differing degrees of shock. When my son-in-law died, for example, I was far more aware of what was happening around me than when my son died. The memories of my son's death and funeral are like a short series of slides flashed onto a screen. I remember certain moments clearly, with painful brilliance, but whatever happened in between was not recorded in my conscious mind. I was behind an opaque veil that lifted briefly on occasion to allow me to record an image—the face of a friend streaming with tears; the casket covered with pale pink roses at the cemetery; the cemetery at sundown, with the same flowers wilted and drooping under the intense summer heat.

RITES OF PASSAGE

Funeral ceremonies are rites of passage that acknowledge to the community that one of its members has died. In the past, the rites of passage for every shift point in life were marked by rituals, which commanded a respected place in our culture. Large extended families came together to honor the person being celebrated. During chaotic times of change and transition, these rituals provided important direction and spiritual strength. There were prescribed ways to behave, and one only had to follow those patterns to gain the support of the community and the comfort of knowing that things were being handled in the correct manner.

Families were much larger in the past, and it was easier for them to come together. They lived close to each other and were more accessible for support and comfort. They didn't relocate often; most kin were born, lived, and died within a few miles of each other.

During the industrial revolution, large families began to break up. Economic necessity drove people to leave farms and small towns to find work in the large cities. Families became smaller, and the rituals that had brought them together in the past were not as functional as they had once been. Rituals took on less importance as time passed, and formal ritual behavior declined throughout our society.

Today, people are increasingly mobile; they look for opportunity beyond a particular community or state or region. In a large city's population, comparatively few people were born there. Distances in our country and even in the world are getting smaller, and it is not unusual for people to live in many places during their lifetime. But this mobility comes with a price.

As our families have grown smaller and our rituals have diminished, so has the level of support we receive during times of transition. Our transitions have little meaning to the group as whole; often, we have to face them alone. Today's watered-down rituals are pale abbreviations in comparison to the rich, faith-filled rituals of the past. The period of time when bereaved people receive support has diminished. Many bereaved people have told me that, after the funeral, friends stopped calling. Interest died down, and people felt awkward in the face of new grief. They tended to stay away from the grieving person and family.

THE VALUE OF FUNERALS AND MEMORIAL SERVICES

I used to think that funerals were "barbaric." I attended them, but I hated every minute. I couldn't see why anyone would submit to such a public ordeal. That was before I went through the many deaths in my family. I think differently now. I have learned the immense value of the spiritual support of friends, and how important they are in helping us as we begin a bereavement. I concede that there are many positive aspects to funerals and memorial services. They include:

◆ Helping to make real a tragic event that would otherwise be easier to deny. Death takes a long time to accept emotionally. Funeral rituals serve to corroborate the fact that a loved one has died and to acknowledge the beginning of bereavement.

◆ Acting to gather friends and family together, thereby providing some support and comfort to the bereaved.

◆ Providing spiritual strength at a time when the bereaved are feeling impoverished emotionally.

◆ Validating the life of the deceased. The rituals are, in the highest sense, a celebration of that life.

◆ Serving to recognize the significant change that has taken place in the lives of the bereaved. The significance of their loss is confirmed.

◆ Giving the bereaved the opportunity to publicly acknowledge their love and devotion for the deceased.

LEAVETAKING RITUALS

There are three phases that emerge over and over again in all ancient rituals. No matter what the purpose of the ritual is, these three phases appear repeatedly:

◆ Severance—that part of the ritual that represents a separation, an ending;

◆ Transition—the phase that represents the slow change from one state to another;

◆ Reincorporation—the phase that acknowledges a re-entry into a new life, a new beginning.

The annual Christian sequence of Maundy Thursday, Good Friday, and Easter Sunday is typically a period that illustrates the three phases.

Some rituals take in only one aspect of the sequence; for example, funerals formalize a *severance,* the *transition* from adolescence to adulthood is marked by an initiation rite, and a marriage signifies an *incorporation* or joining.

These examples show that not all rituals must be forced into a three-part structure. However, the most effective rituals turn out to be structured this way, probably because they reflect universal rhythms. We seem to grow through a series of endings and beginnings with periods of uncertainty in between.

If the analysis of three phases is true, the funeral marks only the first phase of bereavement—separation. What about rituals that could help us through the other two phases? If we are left hanging after the separation phase, what is offered to help us build hope into our lives as we desperately try to believe that the pain will someday subside?

Our society doesn't offer much to bridge the empty months—or even years—of grief, nor does it mark the end of bereavement with celebration and reincorporation. An exception to this is found in the Jewish religion. Bereavement begins with a week of Shiva, during which the family sits together in weeping and extreme sorrow. Everyone is excused from work and given this time to deal with their shock and loss. Acknowledgment points are marked each week during the first month and each month thereafter until the year's end, when a celebration of the reincorporation of the bereaved back into the mainstream of the community is held.

In contemporary primitive tribes, such as the Trobriand Islanders living off the coast of New Guinea, mourning rituals are highly stylized. This is a matrilineal society: descent, kinship, and all social relationships are legally linked through the mother only. However, marriage is patrilocal among the Trobriands—the husband is master of the household. When a woman marries, she moves to her husband's village and lives in his house. This apparent ambiguity of the wife's lineage versus the husband's house nonetheless creates a balance that allows greater power and freedom to the wife.

When a man dies, his wife is far from free of the event. We would expect this to be a time of support from the husband's side of the family. Instead, it works in opposition. The kinsmen fall under a taboo and must keep apart from the corpse. They believe that if they were to touch or come near it, evil influences from the body would attack them, causing disease and death.

The wife then becomes the chief mourner and must make an ostentatious and dramatic display of grief from the moment of death until many months afterward.

A few hours after the death, the body is laid in a grave, dug by the sons or other relatives. The grave is not closed at this time. Rather, a small platform is placed in the grave, over the body, for the widow to lie on during this first night. Surrounding the grave are the kinswomen and friends. It is here that the wake is held.

On the following evening, the body is exhumed for the first time and inspected for signs of sorcery. This is most important: clues may be disclosed as to who caused the death and why.

When the body is again buried, the widow faces her longest trial. She moves into a small cage built within her house, and remains there for months, never leaving, speaking only in whispers, not allowed to touch food and drink with her hands. She must be cared for by others. Her body is smeared with soot and grease, which are not washed off until her mourning is over. This length of time varies but could last anywhere from six months to two years.

Finally, at a time determined by the dead man's kinsmen, she is released from the taboo of confinement and, with appropriate ritual, is requested to walk out of her house. She is ceremoniously washed and anointed, dressed in a new, gaudy, three-color grass skirt, and pronounced, once more, eligible to marry.

We can be glad we don't live among the Trobriands. Yet, several parts of their ritual strike me as beneficial:

◆ The widow knows when her mourning period has ended;
◆ She knows her community will welcome her back;
◆ She has some assurance that she will remarry;

◆ All her guilt has been worked through;
◆ Her anger is spent as well.

The rituals provide the Trobriand widow with a full knowledge of what is expected of her, and she in turn knows what to expect of her community. She is confident that they will care for her, support her, and, at the end of her bereavement, celebrate with her. She is not placed in the "widow" category for the rest of her life, as she would be if she were in America.

How can we offer the same qualities of support to bereaved people in our society? How can we begin to use our rites of passage in a more beneficial and effective manner?

We are desperately in need of new mourning rituals. We are confined to one funeral or memorial service, which usually takes place before the mourning process has really begun. We need rituals more aligned with the evolvement of the process of bereavement. I don't suggest doing away with the initial rituals—the wake, funeral, and burial. These are important functions. I do feel that we need to add more bereavement rituals that would help us along our way and give meaning to our painful passage.

I believe that smaller, community-supported rituals would offer tremendous benefit. In Alcoholics Anonymous, a fantastically effective support and rehabilitative program, the individual receives various colored "chips" to mark his or her progress of abstinence. This is usually done amid the applause and congratulations of his or her compatriots. The expectation for sobriety is strengthened. The journey is marked.

Although we don't have a widespread national support program for bereaved people, any number of smaller groups meeting throughout the country could and do operate in the same supportive manner. There is no question that we need to be helped and encouraged along the painful journey of bereavement. It becomes harder and takes much longer when we attempt it alone.

Some of us don't do well in groups. Our preference is more toward one or two trusted friends. This preference should not stop us from benefiting from the power of rituals. When we can draw spiritual power into our individual experience, we begin to gather strength both psychologically and intellectually. Rituals can help. Their function is to fulfill two human needs that are more basic even than the need for food—the need for meaning in our lives, and the need to belong. They become especially important when life's meaning has been diluted by our final separation from a dearly loved person.

PLANNING A RITUAL OF OUR OWN

Virginia Hine, the noted author and one of my best friends, wrote about rituals in her book, *Rites of Passage for Our Time: A Guide for Creating Rituals:*

> The need for rites of passage at various points in the life cycle is not just a desire to celebrate a change. The comments made repeatedly by people creating such rituals make it clear that self-generated rites of passage also invest the change with meaning it would not otherwise have. Human beings can handle even deeply traumatic experiences if these events are given socially supported positive meaning. In addition, these home-made rituals are performing some of the functions of their ancient precedents—providing the psychological and spiritual power to make the required personal transformations occur in fact.

Rituals of our own making might be very confusing at first. Where do we begin? How can we develop relevant rituals that give expression and meaning to our individualistic spirit? We hope that the rituals will not only help us prepare for, deal with, and commemorate our losses but will also help us inaugurate our new beginning. At the same time, we need to expand our sense of genuine community. We desperately need others to participate in our lives. Self-made rituals can include supportive other people. We won't be alone.

Each of us has probably devised our own ritual at one time or another. Sometimes we do it without realizing what we are doing. When I was eight, my best friend Mary Lou and I became "blood sisters" by pricking our own fingers and then touching them together. We felt really joined at that time, and we believed our ritual created a lasting bond between us.

Joining my sorority had the three phases of a ritual. After going through pledging (severance from others who were not in the sorority) and rough initiation (transition), we were at last formally brought into the group (reincorporation) at a candle-lit "swearing-in." The community then welcomed us. I remember the seriousness of the experience and the high degree of commitment I felt to my sisters and the sorority itself.

Those celebrations were joyous experiences. What about bereavement? Why would we want to devise a personal ritual that deals with sadness and grief? The answer is simple: rituals are *internal* rites of passage that can revitalize our beliefs and attitudes and give fresh meaning to our lives at a time when meaning has been taken from us. Rituals can help us focus on what is and what can be, rather than what was. They can enhance our expectations and set into motion new beginnings.

Devising Our Rituals

What is our main reason for needing to perform a ritual? Is it a separation from something or someone? Is it to mark the transition phase of our major change? Is it to establish a new beginning? Or is it all three?

In bereavement, the severance or separation is usually ritualized with the funeral or memorial service. This marks the beginning of our mourning and gives us permission to express our grief.

What if we are not able to attend the funeral? What if we are in another part of the country and cannot get to the services? In those circumstances, it might be helpful to devise a ritual that depicts our feeling of separation. A woman who was living in California was not physically able to attend her son's funeral in Massachusetts. With the help of a few close friends, she was able to have a small service in her own home.

She knew what the function of the ritual was, so the next question she needed to ask herself was what symbols would be meaningful. She put two recent snapshots of her son into a folding frame, side-by-side, and displayed them for the group. She placed his last letter to her, written several weeks before, nearby. She wrote a letter to him, relating what his life had meant to her and telling him good-bye. Then she asked each of the friends who had known him to write a brief summary of what he had meant to them and to add a special memory they held of him. She found a reading from Kalil Gibran's *The Prophet,* on "Children." A candle represented the spiritual connection. Fresh flowers were arranged in a bowl to depict his beautiful life.

The next day, friends gathered in her living room around her wheelchair. On a small table were placed the photographs, the flowers, and the single candle, which she lit. The ritual began with the reading of a commemorative message by each friend. Then the mother read her letter of good-bye to her son. All the letters were then placed on the table in front of the pictures while a favorite piece of music was played. At the end of the music, the mother folded all the notes, placed them in the folding frame with her son's photographs, and closed the frame, laying it down on the table. (These were to be used in a ritual of reincorporation at a later time.) She then blew out the candle. After a short prayer, they all moved into the dining room to share the food that had been brought by her friends.

This woman told me that it was extremely painful to plan this ritual. She wondered whether she would even be able to go through with it. Because of the form and structure that she had given it, she was able to move through each part with greater calm than she had anticipated. Afterward, there was a distinct feeling that she had been able to say good-bye to her son and that his spiritual presence had been felt by everyone there. "It was a holy time," she said. "God and my son were there together."

Questions About Rituals

I have drawn heavily from the work of Virginia Hine in this discussion of self-made rituals. She suggests that we need to ask ourselves several questions, before we embark on our personal ritual building.

◆ What is the primary function of the ritual?

We can use rituals to help us move through the shock of separation, the confusing transition phase of middle bereavement, or the time when we feel we are ready to move on toward a new identity.

◆ What symbols would be most meaningful?

A variety of components may be combined in planning a ritual. The ascending smoke from candles has long been viewed as representing contact with the world of the spirit. Smoke, especially from incense, is used as a symbol of purification. Because music speaks directly to the transpersonal level of awareness, special songs or words can evoke meaning for the participants. Prayer is a way of focusing intent and directing spiritual awareness. Readings, ritual silence, chanting, and feasting are all means of symbolizing the expression of our feelings.

◆ Whom do we want to be with us?

Private rituals can be very effective and useful. However, a small gathering, enhanced by

mutuality of belief, is a symbolic statement of
spiritual power.

◆ What do we want to say and who will say it?

Speaking aloud is a powerful reinforcement
of personal commitment to change. When our
commitment is shared with others, it becomes
an even greater affirmation of the ritual to be
observed. The assignment of roles will depend
on how many people are involved.

◆ What order would be most effective?

Much will depend on the mood we wish to
create. It is usually best to begin with an affirmation of our purpose. This could be done in a
chant or prayer by all the participants, or could
be read by one person. The order should always
be designated ahead of time.

◆ Where do we want to hold our ritual and
when?

Places may be symbolic of the event or relationship that is being ritualized. Sometimes it
is important to be outdoors, sometimes in-
doors. Anniversaries, certain phases of the
moon, sunrise, or sunset may be important in
the planning process. Time and place may not
be significant, but their symbolism is an important factor to keep in mind.

THE POWER OF SELF-GENERATED RITUALS

There is no way to be uninvolved in a ritual that we have
helped to create. The power of the personal ritual lies both
in its creation and its performance. Once we have invested
ourselves in planning the ritual and developing the meaning
we wish to convey, we are well into tapping a powerful
source of available power and energy.

When we work seriously with others in symbolic reality,
we begin to connect on the transpersonal level. We have the

opportunity to establish bonds that release short bursts of energy into our lives. Perhaps most important of all, rituals are a way of bringing others into our lives, into our crises, and into our healthy renewal. We can reframe our particular circumstances into a positive situation.

Finally, rituals require that we surrender, that we give ourselves over to a process that we ourselves have set into motion. In surrendering, we find that we can let down our barriers and trust that the outcome will be good.

Keeping Rituals Simple

Simple rituals can carry the same power as more complicated ones. The planting of a tree can represent the continuation of life through the transformation of change. I had two wonderful little animals for fifteen years, Liesl, a tiny black dachshund, and Nietzsche, a not-so-tiny black cat. They were best friends to each other as well as constant companions to me. When old age claimed them and they died a week apart, I was bereft. They had been like two little children in my life. Herschel and I buried them with all their little toys at our Florida home, beside the lake where they had walked with me and played together. We planted an evergreen tree over their graves to commemorate their lives and symbolically represent the continuation of love in our hearts.

Thelma, a sixty-two-year-old widow, after grieving for nearly two years, realized that the time had come to let go of her husband. She had spent the entire winter pondering it, trying to think of ways she could begin to put it into motion. She knew she didn't want to let go but she recognized how useless her own life had become. After careful deliberation, on the second anniversary of her husband's death, she devised her ritual.

Her husband had a yellow fishing cap that he used to wear all the time. She had left it hanging on a hook by the back door and had taken comfort that a part of him was still there. On that day, Thelma wrote a letter to him, telling him that she was going to release him. She wrote that they both needed to move on, that their love would always be precious and she would never be without it, but that she had to begin anew. She was still alive and she must do something with her new life.

Thelma took his yellow hat, her letter, and a small cassette player to a deserted section of a nearby beach. She had the area all to herself that day. There, as the sun began to set, she read the letter aloud. When she was finished, she tore it into tiny pieces and tossed it on the water, to be carried out to sea. She then threw her husband's cap out on the waves and, as she watched it disappear toward the horizon, she played a favorite song of theirs, "Memories." Thelma watched the yellow cap bob on the waves until it became a tiny speck. When she could see it no longer, she turned from the water and left. When she got home that evening, she was surprised to find that a weight had been lifted from her shoulders. After two years, she felt released and ready to begin her new life. She said that it was amazing how her energy began to flow in, once she surrendered to the power of her ritual.

Many of our special events and life transitions need to be acknowledged—puberty, divorce, retirement, healing, the dedication of a new home and the departure from a familiar one. Whether rituals are elaborate or simple doesn't matter. What matters is our own involvement. When we give importance to the painful and pleasurable situations we encounter, recognizing them as part of life, the yin and yang, the dark and light, we are acknowledging the fullest expression of what it means to be alive. We cannot control the outcome of experiences that come to us, but we can give them deeper meaning and gain power over their adversities if we don't run from them. Facing realities with meaningful rituals will grant us the strength to face the next difficult time. As our expectations of positive outcomes grow, we have a better chance of creating the reality that we want and deserve.

12

Transcending Grief—Alive Again

How do we transcend grief? As we view it in contemporary America, grief is seen as such a despicable ordeal that it is difficult to imagine that we can even *survive* grief. While I was going through my own bereavements, I had trouble conceiving of ever being without pain. I'm not sure I even wanted to be without misery; it seemed appropriate that I should suffer. If my loved ones couldn't enjoy living, why should I?

Yet, over time, grief gradually changed me. I've come to believe that if we can face the many lessons that bereavement offers us, we can finally triumph over sorrow. We have choices over how we will survive our significant losses. We can choose to maintain a bitterly cynical viewpoint, remaining in the conservation/withdrawal phase of grief, or we can confront the lessons of grief, painful as they are, and treat them instead as opportunities for our growth. When we have the courage to do the latter, we have opted for a triumphant survival. Grief can then lift us up to new plateaus of living and loving. We are capable of deeper, richer relationships, immeasurable compassion, and an extraordinary ability to open our arms to life and adventure. When this happens, like the reshaping of iron forged in red-hot fire, we transcend our grief and its pain.

Joanne's son died when he was only five months old—a crib death. Her husband, John, found the baby cold and blue one morning, when it was his turn to give him the six o'clock bottle. Frantically, John held that little body next to his own, trying to warm him, trying to give him life, as Joanne hysterically called 911. They learned later that the baby had been dead at least two hours. Joanne had been up with him at three o'clock and he was fine. How could he be OK one minute and dead the next? What did they do wrong? What had Joanne done to him when she gave him a bottle at two-thirty, or was it one-thirty? Her mind searched in frenzy for reasons, but there was no explaining this tragic nightmare. How could they transcend their loss?

John and Joanne suffered a long, complicated bereavement. Their anger and guilt kept them from resolution for several years, and they blamed each other in many ways. When they were unable to conceive again, their grief was further complicated. Joanne felt that she was being punished by God. Still, John and Joanne kept trying, with the help of counseling, to adjust to their strange new world together. Eventually, they came to accept the fact that they would never have children of their own. They forgave God and themselves, and they determined to focus on enriching their own relationship as well as supporting and caring for others.

As so often happens, however, shortly after they gave up on ever having another child and accepted the fact that they would be barren, Joanne got pregnant. Overjoyed, they were now ready to welcome a different baby and allow their dead son a place of his own. Fortunately, they had given up their earlier frantic push for success and had settled for a simpler, quieter life. Their daughter Trina is now three years old and never became a replacement baby. John and Joanne felt a stronger and deeper love than they had ever imagined was possible.

LOVE: THE GUIDING FORCE

Love is, I believe, the guiding force of all of life. We concern ourselves with how we give it and how we use it, but mainly with how we get it. We search for reassurances of love from the significant people in our lives. We may think that the way to get love and to feel sustained is to get someone else to love us. If we do favors or services for others they will love us, will not leave us, and will make us secure in their love forever. That kind of exchange has its price. We have to keep doing more things, better things, more often, to continue receiving the rewards. Eventually, we grow weary and usually ask ourselves, "What do I get out of this? I'm not really appreciated, or loved, and after I did all those things, I'm entitled to be loved." This is the point where we begin to develop a bitterness about love. If we had any trust to begin with, we start to lose it now. Some people call this cautious trust *wisdom*. I call it a blind alley, because it leads nowhere, except to further disillusionment.

Grief teaches us that love doesn't work that way. Louise was a very caring, dedicated wife and mother of two daughters, ages twelve and seventeen. Louise tirelessly and willingly took care of everyone at home and managed time for some church duties as well: choir, Sunday school teaching, several committees. She seemed to thrive on these activities, apparently never stopping to consider what *she* needed. As she told me later, "If my family was happy, then so was I."

One day, everything changed. Sally, her older daughter, was on a school picnic at a nearby lake. A good swimmer, she dove off a boat into murky water, not realizing the water was only four feet deep in that place. Her neck was broken and she died on the way to the hospital.

I saw Louise in therapy about six months after the accident. She was filled with terrible guilt and shame; she felt that she was, in many ways, responsible for Sally's death. Pain was communicated in every word and movement. She sobbed deeply as she tried to share her feelings that morning:

> What have I done wrong? I've tried to be a good mother . . .
> worked hard in my church. Goodness knows, I've taken care
> of my husband and given him a good home. I thought I was

doing things right but . . . nothing has worked out. How
could God punish me when I tried so hard?

Her sobs took her breath away for a moment. She continued
when she could control her voice a little better.

It is so hard to admit this but I truly believe if I'd been taking
care of Sally this would not have happened. I didn't want her
to go on that picnic. She needed to study for exams. Sally
had gotten behind these last two weeks. I told her so but she
just wouldn't listen. . . . Oh God, why am I being punished like this? What have I done? I don't know anybody else
whose child was killed. Why mine?

These questions were a constant torment for her. Reassurance that she wasn't to blame had little effect. Her shame
and guilt could not be abated.

Several years passed before Louise could release the guilt
and learn to forgive herself. She began to realize that she
had looked to others for approval and self-worth. She had
searched for love in the wrong places. Our search for love
will continue until we come to love ourselves. When we can
understand our own worth, we'll no longer doubt ourselves
and we'll be free to love and understand others in a deeper
way.

Changing was an enormous risk for Louise, as it is for
most of us. What if no one would love her? What if no one
needed her? Somehow, these questions became academic after the tragic loss she had sustained. Finally, Louise had to
admit that she had been too busy before Sally's death to do
a good job with anything; she had given only partial attention to any one thing and had always been afraid to cut
anything out.

Louise began to take the time to develop herself. She took
some courses at the local college, reserved time for meditation, and spent more time at home just *being with* her husband and daughter. As she let go of her strong desire to
please others, she discovered what joy could come from

pleasing herself. She began to say "No" to the things she didn't want to do or had no time to do. She began to structure some of the things she had put off doing for herself—the pottery class at the art center, the long postponed exercise class. As she became more gentle and loving toward herself, she became more tolerant and loving toward others. When Louise began to slow her pace, she had more time to calmly interact with her world. She felt filled with love for the universe, and that love overflowed toward everyone around her.

Louise will always miss Sally terribly, but now she remembers her in the sweetness of love rather than the internal blackness of guilt. Changing the perception of herself helped her change the perception of her whole world. She allowed love to work in and through her, rather than focusing on the drudgery of duty and the need for outside approval to rule her life.

THE LESSONS OF GRIEF

There are many lessons to be learned before we can approach a place of transcendence. In the early phases of grief, when we are grappling with disappointment, anger, and loss, life's lessons may not be what we have chosen to learn. However, I firmly believe everything that comes our way is material for our growth. I have a hard time accepting that loss comes to us only to teach us, but I believe that when we suffer a loss we are presented with challenges that enhance our growth—*if* we are willing to see them that way.

When life is good, there is a tendency to become complacent about our surroundings. We are prone to take things for granted. John, a fifty-five-year-old widower, said that he wished he could live his marriage over again. "I would have complimented Josie more, done things for her, seen all the places we had dreamed about together. . . . Now it's too late. She's gone." Our appreciation of the true values of living gets lost in our rush to get through the tasks of the day. We somehow expect there will be no real traumas.

Grief teaches us to stop and examine what we truly want from life—the values that so often get pushed into the background but offer us the richness and texture of living that our souls deeply crave. When we recapture these values, we are spiritually sustained.

The Value of Living in the Present

Grief teaches us the importance of living in the present. We realize, after losing someone dear, the value of every precious moment. Living in the present means that we let go of the past and all its hurts, but it also means that we must not live in the future. Keeping control, trying to plan the outcome of all our events, only leaves us tied up in our own ego and defenses. Time is not on our side, and we need to experience life as it is presented to us. When we become willing to enjoy the moment, we find hidden treasures everywhere— the thrilled expression on a child's face while watching a kite ascend, or a flower in full bloom, or the rarefied colors of a summer sunrise as the sky opalesces from pale pink to brilliant gold. These are treasures worth searching for, but we must be willing to be here, in the present moment, to truly experience their wonder.

The Joy of Spontaneity

Grief teaches us the joy of spontaneity. We are aware more than ever of the need to take advantage of opportunities to play or relax. We learn that we must not waste chances to have lighthearted fun. If we keep to a rigid schedule, we miss the serendipity that is all around us. Life may be predictable when lived that way, but it becomes stagnant and boring. We need to accept the freedom of spontaneity as our right and privilege.

The Value of Time

There is a sweet beauty about life that we all try to grasp and hold on to. We feel the need, from time to time, to go back over the innocent moments of our lives. We want to deal with the questions of life and love—and even of death. We promise ourselves that we will do some soul searching when we have time. Then we keep busy with constant daily distractions so that we can excuse ourselves for putting off any opportunity for learning to center ourselves. What we come to realize only later is that these questions are answered for us in many hidden ways, if we would only take the time to find them. Valuable insights are buried in the give and take of daily life; if we could slow ourselves down, we could find them. We all need what I call "hammock time"—experiences of daydreaming and fantasy. We need time to share our feelings with one another, but first we need to know what our feelings are. Grief teaches us that there is much to know about ourselves and our world, but that kind of knowledge requires a slower perception. We get hints of the wonders that are possible, when we have occasional peak experiences. Slowing our lives would offer us many more of those wonders.

The Need for Simplicity

Only after we have something taken from us do we realize its true value. We usually find that, because we spend so much energy trying to take care of the details of living, we miss many of life's smaller but important transactions. Ann realized, only after she had lost her husband, how much time she had wasted every day constantly prodding her husband to keep the house neat. Now it didn't matter how the house looked. She wished she had spent her time enjoying him rather than cleaning all the time. Grief teaches us that we need to simplify our lives so that more time is available for sharing with those we love.

We get caught up in daily distractions that take too much energy. To do things perfectly, we complicate our lives and add needless stress. Our perfectionism is a function of our egos and has no place in the world of love. Learning to live more simply frees our energies to be truly creative. In a world full of stimulation, it is necessary to divest ourselves of as many needless tasks as we can. Generally, we become more efficient in order to get more tasks accomplished in a day. What if we were to simplify everything as much as we could, and then used that time to be more creative? How our souls would be regenerated and our spirits uplifted!

The Benefits of Change

Without change, we wither and die. Roger felt locked into a job he hated. Being a highly responsible person, he thought his first duty was to provide for his family. Secretly, he dreamed of quitting his miserable job and starting a lawn service, which would allow him to be outside all the time. He thought about it incessantly but could never figure out how to do it. He couldn't even bring himself to talk to his wife about it. Instead, he stuck with his job for twenty-three years, growing more lifeless with each year.

When he got colon cancer, he had a lot of time to review his life. He vowed that, if he could get strong again, he would start his little business. Even thinking about it made him feel freer. He didn't care how he did it; he knew he would be a success.

Recovery after surgery was slow, but gradually he was able to put his plan into operation. He contracted for only a couple of yards to start with; as he gained strength, he was able to add more. The last time I talked with Roger, he had no sign of the cancer and was happier than he had ever been.

Either we grow or we regress. There is no in-between, no status quo in life. Yet, we continue to resist change with all the strength we can muster. It has been said that we go kicking and screaming to our growth. Facing change is one of the hardest lessons of grief. Who wants loss? We didn't want it and we haven't asked for it. But it has come to us, and somehow we must deal with it. We don't have many choices: either we keep on or we give up. If we give up, our soul dies. If we keep on, we roll with the changes, whatever they may be, and try to keep faith that we will come through. Grief teaches us that we must trust our higher power to lead us on the right path, to give us perfect guidance even when we lose sight of it or reject its effects.

The Value of Patience

How frustrated we become when we must wait for something to happen. We like to have control over our world, to make things happen when we want them to happen, rather than leaving life to another set of rules. Grief teaches us that life can't be hurried if we expect to get out of it the best it offers. Patience helps us to seek out an understanding of each other, to wait good-humoredly when others must catch up. Grief also teaches us that we must be patient with ourselves, allowing the grieving process to take place in whatever manner it is supposed to. If life becomes hurried, we miss the best part—the quiet, uneventful, deeply meaningful moments we can know alone or with those we love.

The Pleasure of Laughter

In his book, *Anatomy of an Illness,* Norman Cousins describes how he cured his fatal illness with laughter. Doctors told him there was little or no treatment for his disease. He had noticed that, if he watched a funny program on TV, he slept better that night and had less pain. Cousins immediately set about to locate old movies and TV shows that made him laugh: "Candid Camera," Marx Brothers films, episodes of "I Love Lucy." He literally laughed himself back to health.

Norman Cousins's book contains an important lesson. When we laugh, our bodies are recharged and every cell is affected. The full, relaxing response of a wonderful belly laugh derives from a powerful physiological reaction that surges throughout the body. We come alive both emotionally and physically.

During grief, we often feel disloyal or guilty when we laugh; it doesn't seem appropriate at such a sad and somber time. Yet, grief is an emotionally charged period. When we laugh, we allow the tension to escape like steam from a simmering tea kettle. Laughter becomes a safety valve against explosion; it ensures better health because it releases some of the tension locked within our bodies.

Choosing to see the funny side as well as the serious side of life heals our pain and encourages wellness. Because it is habit-forming and contagious, laughter shared with others can heal them as well as ourselves.

The Need to Belong

Our need to belong to someone or something is as old as time itself. Our sense of belonging to the human race and our recognition of the importance of our kinship to each other enhance our quality of life. Grief teaches us that we need others. Over and over, bereaved people have told me that having friends near, feeling a closeness to them, being a part of a group, were all sustaining forces when they faced their personal tragedies. We need a sense of belonging—to the neighborhood, the folks who work with us, the group we call our friends. Knowing that we belong helps us feel more secure, more a part of the human race.

One of the wonderful things about bereavement support groups is that our pain can be shared with people who know what we are feeling. I heard one man say at a Compassionate Friends meeting, "I know when I come here I belong—no one will judge me . . . we're all in the same boat." Knowing that others have survived equally devastating experiences gives us courage and hope. Suffering softens us and helps us to feel more compassion toward one another. Grief teaches us that we need to be more connected with others in our world. We learn the importance of keeping those connections alive.

The Value of Sharing

One of grief's lessons is the importance of being open, of candidly sharing our thoughts and feelings. As a therapist dealing with bereaved people, I often hear the phrase, "I wish I had been able to say, 'I love you.'" Or, "Dad never knew I had forgiven him. I was waiting for the right time to talk with him." There may be things we need to say, appreciations we should express, separations that we should close. Grief teaches us that we have only *now* to let other persons know we love them. Families that stay open, sharing their feelings whether hot or cold, trust each other more readily and survive losses with less guilt or ambivalence than families living with barriers.

There is magic in sharing ourselves with someone else. Each of us profits from hearing another's story. We need to recognize and celebrate our bond with others.

If we haven't been as open as we'd like, one phone call can begin rectifying the situation. When we become more open and share ourselves honestly with others, they begin to follow suit. Sharing is as contagious as laughter.

The Need to Expand Our Family of Choice

As we get older, we find ourselves in an ever diminishing circle of family and friends. This happens particularly after our children are grown. There seem to be fewer opportunities to form new relationships. Our children were often emissaries who brought new friends (and their parents) into our lives.

As we begin to lose our dearest friends through death or distances and we see our own families diminish in number, we have an increasing need to gather in new "family members" of our own choice.

We can adopt new family members any time we find non-related kin—those special people who come into our lives as strangers but seem to have been friends all our lives.

I love a story Isabella Taves tells in her book, *Love Must Not Be Wasted*. Davis was three when his grandfather died. His grandmother told him Gramps had gone to heaven and was happy with the angels. A few weeks later, he told his mother that he would like to go over to his grandmother's and see whether Gramps was back from heaven.

David's mother, who had never approved of the heaven concept, tried to explain that Gramps was dead and buried and could not return. David wanted to know if that would happen to Grandma, too. His mother explained that all of us die. David went down a long list of people in the family, asking if each one would die. Then he asked about his beloved collie. Finally, he said, "And you, Mommy?" His mother said yes, she would die too, but not for a long time, not until David was grown up.

David thought a minute before announcing, "Then I guess I'll have to get me a new set of people."

Grief teaches us that we need to keep reaching out to others, to get a new set of people when we find our own set growing smaller. If we do this, we will never be lonely or feel excluded from life.

The Worth of Relationships

There is a lot of talk about the risk involved in loving. For anyone who loves and therefore risks forming a connection with another person, suffering is guaranteed. But only when we love will we find a fullness of life and a personal experience of tremendous satisfaction.

Grief teaches us that relationships can never be taken for granted. People come into our lives to teach us, and each person is a special gift to be treasured and never taken for granted. Some people seem to be placed into our lives as comforters who help us to get through: special friends, resource people, family members who weren't close or available before. When we finally reach the other side of grief and are on our way to a new life, we may find strangers who become like family. We can only find them if we stay open to other people.

TRANSCENDENCE

Aware of a New Self

As we practice grief's lessons, we slowly begin to transcend our bereavement. We change. We come to see grief as a death-and-resurrection experience. We become aware that a part of us has died and another part is being reborn.

We can trust our inner yearnings to lead us in our rebirth. Naturally, we will have some trepidation because of the risks ahead. We may find it difficult to accept our new self; we don't feel "normal." But we have come to know that, with help from providence, we are moving on toward restored strength and renewed energy.

Alive to a New World

After the sorrow and sadness we have felt in grief, we are ready to face our resurrection experience. We are on a journey in this life that is bringing us closer to full understanding of the joy that can be possible within each sorrowful situation. When we have aligned ourselves with our higher power, and have sought love in our relationships with others and with the universe, we are gifted with love in bountiful return. Every single minute has something for us, a new piece of information, a missing part of our life-puzzle, an idea that resolves a perplexing dilemma, an insight into peace. This *is* a new world, with new possibilities.

I am reminded of a couple who were my close friends in Florida. Martha and Charles were both eighty-four when Charles died. Their marriage had been one of continuing romance, sometimes tempestuous but always interesting and fun. We couldn't imagine one partner without the other; for a while, we worried that the outlook for Martha's bereavement would be bleak. Yet, it didn't surprise anyone when she decided to write a daily newspaper column on grief and loss and encouraged readers to send letters to her. The column became so popular that it was syndicated throughout the country. Martha kept her column going until her death six years later! No matter what age we are, it is never too late to begin anew.

More Adventurous

We have been through the dark, despairing days of grief and have realized that continuing in that mood state can be an addiction. Our decision to move from the conservation/withdrawal phase to the healing phase gives our lives a new perspective. No longer must we dwell in the predictable, dull time of no movement. Keeping our minds closed and our attitudes and behavior rigid means death to our human spirit.

Life's joys rest in adventure. When we are alert in the here and now, we are constant collectors of new information. We're promised adventure every moment if we open our hearts to it. When we accept new possibilities, we make better decisions, have new opinions, achieve advanced enlightenment. Life becomes freer and much more fun!

More Curious

Two powerful characteristics have been found in people who have long, successful, and happy lives. One is a strong sense of adventure and the other is a healthy curiosity. Curiosity becomes a powerful guard against complacency and stagnation. When we are curious about our world, we tend to push our boundaries, constantly expanding our ability to perceive things from many different vantage points.

As we get older, there is a tendency to try to make our lives as safe as possible. We restrict ourselves to ideas and people similar to our own. Our world becomes smaller and more rigid. We stop growing.

The antidote is a strong, natural, instinctive curiosity. Children have it because we are born with it. When we maintain our curiosity, we are guaranteed that our lives will never be dull or uninteresting.

Curiosity supplies us with the desire to push our boundaries, question ideas, seek new information. A willingness for adventure gives us the spirit to act on new ideas and interests.

Better Risk Takers

Through some miracle, we have been brought through the dark tunnel of grief. We have learned to let go and allow our higher power to carry us. We now know that we are always taken care of, right here, right now. Recognizing this eases our anxieties and erases our fears.

Fears keep us immobilized. To fully reap the benefits that life offers us, we need to be willing to risk full exposure to what any moment offers. Living in the present gives us ample opportunity to practice taking risks.

Life holds dangers as well as rewards. We choose how we will act. When we allow a power greater than ourselves to guide us, we become freer individuals. The same world we feared in the past now becomes our classroom for learning how to become all that we dare to become.

More Compassionate

We have learned a deeper sense of compassion. Having experienced the humbling pain of grief, we can more readily sympathize with this pain in others.

We are climbing the same mountain, all of us. We will cross paths now and then and we can be grateful for all the intersections. Any path that we cross makes a special contribution to our own progress. There are no accidents in life. Because each person brought into our lives can teach us, we welcome all persons with compassion and understanding. We find spiritual strength through touching the souls of one another.

Grateful for Each Day

Gratitude prepares us for blessings that are to come. In the past, there were days when we were desperate with yearning for our lost loved one to return. We didn't have the vision to see ahead. We didn't care about the future. There didn't seem to be much to be grateful for.

Many blessings have helped to guide our way since our grief began. Somehow, we survived. Looking back, we recognize the many supports we were offered along the way. Sometimes we still feel buried in sand—blocked, clogged, unable to move. Then we remember that we are not alone. Help is at hand if only we will ask for it.

To awaken each morning with thoughts of praise and gratitude prepares us for the blessings of the day. Going to sleep at night provides an opportunity to recount the blessings of the day and give thanks for them. When we acknowledge our gifts, we prepare the way for inner peace.

When we fill our lives with gratitude, we invoke a self-fulfilling prophecy. What we expected to happen does happen. The self-fulfilling prophecy works. Our lives are richly blessed.

More Loving

We come to learn, through the lessons of grief, the supreme importance of loving others. Love has many wonders. Love is a healing balm for our wounds. Love nurtures both the one being loved and the one who is loving. It is an energizer spurring us on to successes in work and play. Love multiplies itself. If we love, our souls will never be hungry.

Jerald Jampolsky, in his wonderful book, *Love Is Letting Go of Fear,* tells us that love is the way to inner peace. He writes:

> With love as our only reality, health and wholeness can be viewed as inner peace, and healing can be seen as letting go of fear.

I said earlier that I believe love to be the guiding force of all life. We are changed through loving and being loved. The receiving of love is often more difficult than the giving. Bereavement teaches us the need to accept whatever is offered in the spirit of love. We learn how uplifting it feels to be loved, especially during grief, when we feel so unlovable and rejected.

Love is a gift to be given and received over and over—a commodity that needs constant attention. Loving and being loved is not just something that happens to us. It is a creative art that must be worked out in a variety of ways. Behind it always is the initial need to love ourselves. Without that, the gift is incomplete.

Spiritual Growth

There have been days in our grief when we felt spiritually deserted, rejected, and shamed by our loss. We wanted to hide. We know now that at the moment when we were able to let go of control, we began to rebuild our trust and faith.

As I have been writing this book, I have become aware of a need to identify a sixth phase of grief: spiritual growth. I believe that we haven't taken theory far enough until we incorporate spiritual fulfillment as the final phase of bereavement. Some people will not opt to enter this phase— but then some will not push to the healing or renewal phase either. We take the steps we can when we are ready for each one. Our spiritual journey continues for a lifetime and even beyond, and it is within our spiritual realm that we find the connection to serenity. Once we have made this connection, wisdom and knowledge are openly accessible to us.

Being faith-filled takes effort. Faith grows with our positive experiences and must endure our negative ones. We need to continue "practicing" in order to foster its growth. Daily meditation keeps us self-directed, but our basic security and safety lie in our relationship with our higher power. Serenity is offered when we are able to seek divine guidance for courage and strength. And yet, many times—because we can't see it, touch it, or hear it—we doubt the sustaining power of our connection to that guidance.

Scott Peck, in his inspiring book, *The Road Less Traveled,* talks of the powerful force that is found in the concept of grace:

> What are we to do—we who are properly skeptical and scientific minded—with this "powerful force originating outside of human consciousness which nurtures the spiritual growth of human beings"? We cannot touch this force. We have no decent way to measure it. Yet it exists. It is real. Are we to operate with tunnel vision and ignore it because it does not fit in easily with traditional scientific concepts of natural law? To do so seems perilous. I do not think we can hope to approach a full understanding of the cosmos, of the place of man within the cosmos, and hence the nature of mankind itself, without incorporating the phenomenon of grace into our conceptual framework.

Grace is given to each of us when we make room for it. Sometimes, grace comes unwelcomed because it brings radical change and upheaval into our lives. We are not always ready to accept grace in these initial forms. Still, we have survived many hard times in our lifetime, and we know they eventually come to an end. Others will probably occur later in our lives but, having practiced the lessons of grief, we are better prepared to deal with them.

There is much to be learned at low tide. Sorrow heightens joy. Depression heightens laughter. If it weren't for our low times, we wouldn't recognize the peaks. Through our sad times, we learn to patiently wait for wisdom to help us see the way.

Reflecting on the painful experiences of our griefs, we realize they have made us wiser. We are not the same people we were. Instead, we are stronger and more capable than we were before our loss.

The difficult times pull us inward and urge us to search for our connectedness to a higher power. Once we have felt the connection, we realize that we are finally at home, at peace with our souls, and holding the gift of serenity at last.

God grant us
  The serenity to accept the things we cannot change,
   The courage to change the things we can,
    And the wisdom to know the difference.
    Amen.

Support Groups That Offer Help

For widowed persons

Parents Without Partners
8807 Colesville Road
Silver Spring, MD 20910
(301) 588-9354

THEOS (They Help Each Other Spiritually)
1301 Clark Boulevard or
717 Liberty Avenue
Pittsburgh, PA 15222
(412) 471-7779

Widowed Persons Service
American Association of Retired Persons
1909 K Street, N.W.
Washington, DC 20049
(202) 872-4700

For parental and sibling bereavement

Candelighters Childhood Cancer Foundation
1901 Pennsylvania Avenue, N.W.
Suite 1001
Washington, DC 20006

The Compassionate Friends
P.O. Box 3696
Oak Brook, IL 60522-3696
(312) 990-0010

MADD (Mothers Against Drunk Drivers)
669 Airport Freeway—Suite 310
Hurst, TX 76053
(817) 268-6233

National Sudden Infant Death Syndrome (SIDS)
8200 Professional Place
Suite 104
Landover, MD 20785

Parents of Murdered Children
100 East Eighth Street
Room B41
Cincinnati, OH 45202
(513) 721-5683

SHARE (Source of Help in Airing and Resolving
    Experiences)
St. John's Hospital
800 East Carpenter
Springfield, IL 62769
(217) 544-6464

References

Bridges, W. (1980). *Transitions: Making Sense of Life's Changes.* Reading, MA: Addison-Wesley Publishing Co., Inc.

Corey, G. (1977). *Theory and Practice of Counseling and Psychotherapy.* Belmont, CA: Wadsworth Publishing Co.

Cousins, N. (1979). *Anatomy of an Illness.* New York: Bantam Books.

Feinstein, D., and Mayo, P. E. (1990). *Rituals for Living and Dying.* San Francisco: Harper & Row.

Herz, F. (1980). "The impact of death and serious illness on the family life cycle." In E. Carter and M. McGoldrick (Eds.), *The Family Life Cycle.* New York: Gardner.

Hine, V., and Foster, S. *Rites of Passage for Our Time: A Guide for Creating Rituals.* Unpublished manuscript.

Jampolsky, G. G. (1979). *Love Is Letting Go of Fear.* Berkeley, CA: Celestial Arts.

Lewis, C. S. (1961). *A Grief Observed.* New York: The Seabury Press.

Malinowski, B. (1929). *The Sexual Life of the Savages.* New York: Harcourt, Brace & World.

O'Neill, N., and O'Neill, G. (1974). *Shifting Gears: Finding Security in a Changing World.* New York: M. Evans & Co., Inc.

Peck, M. S. (1979). *The Road Less Traveled.* New York: Simon & Schuster.

Rando, T. A. (1988). *Grieving: How to Go on Living When Someone You Love Dies.* Lexington, MA: Lexington Books.

Sanders, C. M. (1989). *Grief: The Mourning After*. New York: John Wiley & Sons.

Schatz, W. H. (1986). "Grief of fathers." In T. A. Rando (Ed.), *Parental Loss of a Child*. Champaign, IL: Research Press.

Taves, I. (1974). *Love Must Not Be Wasted*. New York: Thomas Y. Crowell Co.

Index

About the Author

Catherine M. Sanders, Ph.D. is a psychologist in clinical practice in Charlotte, North Carolina, specializing in individuals who have suffered a traumatic loss. She has done extensive research into the effects of bereavement of both individuals and families. Her work in the field dates back to 1968 when she began construction of the Grief Experience Inventory, a multidimensional measure of the grief experience and process used both in this country and internationally in research and clinical situations.

After completing her Ph.D. at the University of South Florida, she founded and was director of the Loss and Bereavement Resource Center where she consulted, provided training programs for professionals, conducted research, and taught graduate courses in death and dying at the University. She received both pre- and post-doctoral research awards from the National Institute of Mental Health to study the effects of bereavement on adults. In addition, she has helped develop a training program for hospice nurses. Dr. Sanders' current research focuses on the process and effects of grief when facing a separation or divorce. She acted as psychological consultant to WBTV in Charlotte, appearing weekly to report on a variety of topics and answer questions from the viewing audience. She has written extensively in the area of bereavement and is author of *Grief: The Mourning After* (Wiley, 1989), which was chosen by the American Library Association as one of the outstanding academic books of the year. She has also written *How to Survive the Loss of a Child: Filling the Emptiness and Rebuilding Your Life,* due in early June, 1992. Dr. Sanders is the recipient of the Association for Death Education and Counseling's 1990 award for her "Outstanding Contribution in the Field of Death-Related Counseling." She is Executive Director and Founder of the Center for the Study of Separation and Loss.